Ian Botham

Ian Botham on Cricket

Photographs by Geoff Goode

CASSELL
LONDON

Cassell Ltd.
35 Red Lion Square, London WC1R 4SG
and at Sydney, Auckland, Toronto, Johannesburg,
an affiliate of
Macmillan Publishing Co., Inc.,
New York

First edition April 1980
First edition, second impression July 1980

ISBN 0 304 30478 6

Printed and bound in Great Britain at
The Camelot Press Ltd, Southampton

Ian Botham on Cricket

Contents

Illustrations

Acknowledgements

I would like to thank my Somerset colleagues Vic Marks, Peter Roebuck, Brian Rose and Derek Taylor for the help they gave me in some of the specialist areas of this book, and also Ralph Ellis, who helped me get my thoughts and ideas down on paper.

Ian Botham

Introduction

I set out to make this book different from any cricket coaching book I have ever seen. I believe that 99 per cent of them belong in the dustbin. They seem to want to turn cricket from the marvellous sport it is into a chess match.

A good cricketer, for me, is one who scores runs, takes wickets and fields well. He is fit, he looks smart, he gives 100 per cent effort, he puts the team first. Most important, he enjoys the game. What his style looks like doesn't matter. Yet somehow most of the books I have seen put appearances first. They concentrate on producing so-called 'stylish' players. I think that is to run the risk of developing cricketers who look magnificent but can't hit the ball off the square.

I love cricket. I turned down the chance to be a professional footballer because I wanted to take my chance as a cricketer. The game is like a drug to me – I want to be always playing it and I love talking about it. When it is raining I prowl around the dressing-room like a caged lion.

More than anything cricket is fun. I enjoy every second that I am on the field, and my first aim in this book is to help others to share that enjoyment. There's nothing to beat the excitement of taking a spectacular catch, or hitting a six, or sending the middle stump cartwheeling.

For me, the appeal of cricket is that you can never beat it. One day you can score a century and take five or six wickets – the next you can get a duck and see your bowling smashed to all parts of the ground. What's more, you can have played badly the first day and well the second. Nobody can guarantee when they walk on to a cricket field that they will do well. I doubt if there has ever been a batsman who could honestly say he has never been out for a duck.

What you can do is reduce the margin of error so that the good days outweigh the bad. That is the principal aim of coaching, and books on coaching. It is what I aim to help you to do, except that I want to tackle the problem in a different way.

Nearly every coaching book I've ever seen lays down exact rules on how to play every shot. They seem to take a perfectly proportioned young boy, and show him the perfect stance and the perfect way to move his feet, arms and body. This is all very well, but how many perfectly proportioned people do you know? Most of the people I have met are either short or tall, fat or skinny, or perhaps uncoordinated to some degree. Perhaps their eyesight might be weak in one eye, or their sense of balance poor. You can be certain that what is right for one is uncomfortable and wrong for another.

If everybody conformed to the traditional books you would end up with a long line of identical mass-produced players. That would make the game horribly boring. Some of the top players in the game are the most unorthodox. Bob Willis, Mike Brearley, Asif Iqbal and Alan Knott are a few examples of top players who defy the traditional text-books in some aspect of their game. There are many others.

Imagine trying to tell Viv Richards that he hadn't played a shot correctly while the ball was whistling to the boundary for four. It would be ridiculous. Yet that is what a lot of school and club coaches do. Instead of saying 'good shot' when a youngster hits the ball hard, they confuse him with all sorts of advice. Before long they can make him afraid to even try and hit the ball.

There are a few basic rules to follow when you play cricket – and from there every player must develop his own style. In this book I am going to concentrate on those basic rules. Follow them and you can enjoy improvising in all sorts of ways – but break them and you will struggle to get anywhere.

I was lucky in that when I joined the Lord's ground staff I was encouraged to play my own way. Harry Sharp, who was the assistant head coach, would stand behind the nets helping me. If I played a shot which was unorthodox, but still came from the middle of the bat and was going for four, he would tell me 'good shot' and leave it at that. He might tell me to follow through with more power, or some minor point, but that would be all, because the basics were correct.

If I played a bad shot, on the other hand, and broke the elementary rules – perhaps lifted my head or didn't use my feet to get to the pitch of the ball – Harry would come down on me like a ton of bricks. He would tell me what was wrong, and how to put it right. He earned my respect for that, and I would always expect to learn from his advice. Harry has since become Middlesex scorer, but we still keep in touch and he still helps me. That, to me, is how coaches should encourage youngsters. Their job is to produce young players who enjoy hitting the ball hard, and knocking the stumps over, but do it safely.

I have always believed in aggressive cricket. As a young boy my idol was Gary Sobers, the former Nottinghamshire and West Indies captain, and I think the greatest all-rounder of all. He played the game the way I try to . . . when he was batting he got on with it and kept the score moving, punishing bad bowling – and when he bowled he could look at the wicket and bowl the most dangerous delivery for the conditions.

He was my idol – but I don't think he influenced me. I have always tried to be Ian Botham, and not another Gary Sobers. For one, there could never be another Gary Sobers, and for another, as I have been trying to explain, you cannot lay down a model for anybody to follow. Everyone has different talents, and has to exploit them to the best of his ability, in his own way. That is what I hope this book will help young cricketers to do.

Chapter 1 **Attitude is all-important**

A good cricketer is aggressive. By that I don't mean he is unpleasant, or a cheat, or that he argues with umpires or opponents. I mean he tries his hardest to take wickets, or score runs, or save runs in the field, committing himself totally to the game and trying to win it. His aim is to put the opposition under unbearable pressure all the time – and then be able to relax and joke with them after the match.

My attitude to the game is simply this. When I am batting the bowler is not good enough, and when I am bowling the batsman isn't good enough. I suppose that makes me sound conceited, but I honestly believe that if everybody adopted that sort of attitude in everything they did – whether they were a cricketer, a doctor, or a roadsweeper – the whole world would flow more easily. I hate to see people not trying, going through the motions of taking part in a game, with their thoughts wandering over all sorts of things entirely unconnected with the match they are playing.

I want to stress again, though, that there is the greatest difference between being aggressive and trying hard, and being unpleasant and temperamental. I hate losing – but I'd be an idiot if I thought I would never be beaten, so I know that when it happens I must be prepared to congratulate the man who beat me.

Cricket is different from almost any other team game in that individual performances stand out. A footballer could play badly, but because his team won it might go unnoticed. In cricket the man who scores a century or takes six wickets stands out as the hero. His team-mate who got a duck has equally obviously failed. So it is natural that everyone wants his own personal performance to be good and wants to be the star of the show. If I were allowed to, I would bowl all through the innings or try to bat all day.

That, I believe, is how to approach the game. Enthusiasm is a vital quality. But just as you must curb your aggression with sportsmanship, it is equally important to remember that the team is more important than the individual. Everything you do on a cricket field is a contribution to the needs of your team, and you must always be ready to sacrifice your own glory for the team to win.

It is in this respect that I think cricket is a great game for youngsters to play. It builds character. You learn to battle when things are against you, to help your team-mates along, to be unselfish in your attitude to others.

Team spirit, the will to put the needs of a given situation in a match before your own wishes, turns defeat into victory. I think the current England team has shown that many times. It is the reason why we field so well and why we have been so successful.

It was brought home to me most in the Fourth Test in Sydney during the 1978–9 tour to Australia. We began the match disastrously; at one time we were 98 for eight in the first innings, but we battled our way back into the match, and eventually won it comfortably and clinched the Ashes.

Twice in that game I had to sacrifice myself for the team. First I had to do an enormous amount of bowling after Mike Hendrick and Bob Willis were forced to go off. They were suffering from intense heat. It was sticky, sweltering and unpleasant – but if I had given less than my best I would have let down myself and, more important, the team.

Then I had to bat at a time when occupying the crease mattered more than scoring runs. Again it was hot, and difficult to bat, and the Australian bowlers were letting the bouncers fly. I don't think I played an aggressive shot in two hours, which is very much against the way I like to play. But I think it went some way towards helping us win the game, and that is what counts.

Equally there are times when Somerset need quick runs – and because of the way I play I am told to try to get them. It means I can't play myself in, or build a big innings, and I might well get out trying to force the pace. But it would be no good to say 'Forget it, I am going to play for my own average', because that would be depriving the team of the chance to win the match. By scoring eight off two balls in the final over with ten required you can contribute just as much as the team-mate who scored eighty earlier in the innings. It may not look so good in the figures at the end of the season, but it will win you just as much respect from your team.

I want to stress again one aspect of the game which is most important. *Never argue with an umpire.* There will be times when you want to, when you are given out unjustly, or have an l.b.w. appeal turned down, or think you have run a batsman out and the umpire doesn't give the decision. But the laws of cricket say that the umpire's decision is final. In other words, no matter how wrong he is, he is right, because nothing will change his decision.

If you stand and complain, you only make yourself look silly. There will be days when the wrong decisions go against you, and days when they are in your favour, and you must accept that. I am not saying it is easy – I will admit there have been times when I wanted to argue. But I didn't and I wouldn't. And grumbling all afternoon to your team-mates isn't going to win you any friends, either. It will ruin their game as well as your own. The umpire has got a job to do, and he will do it to the best of his ability.

Your attitude to the game is all-important. It decides how much enjoyment you get. Try hard, be unselfish and be a good sportsman, and you will get plenty.

Chapter 2 **Eyes on the ball**

The first rule of playing any game is to watch the ball. In cricket, where concentration counts for so much, it is doubly important. Every delivery, every over, every session, every day, you have to concentrate on the ball.

For a start, there is nothing more certain than that the moment you let your mind wander elsewhere the game will be unkind to you. You can stand in the slips and do nothing all day – but it is odds-on that the one ball you let your mind wander from will be the one that brings a catching chance. For some reason that seems to apply to wherever you field. Fall asleep and the ball will find you out. The only answer is to watch it all the time.

It is difficult, I know. A lot of people can concentrate for an hour, or two, but then they get tired and can't give the game enough attention any more. If you are like that then I do sympathize, because I used to be the same. My mind would start to drift all over the place, and it would end with the captain getting annoyed with me. I can see some of the younger players in the county game doing the same thing now. It is all a matter of applying yourself and it can be overcome.

How you conquer the concentration barrier is an individual thing. Some people chew gum, others talk, others keep quiet. Some talk to themselves. My personal way is to switch off the moment the ball is dead. I concentrate totally from the moment the bowler starts his run until the ball is dead – then I relax completely and have a chat and a joke with another fielder. But as soon as the bowler reaches his mark I switch back on to the game. I think anybody who can concentrate totally all the time is inhuman. I certainly can't. So I try to keep the light moments to times when they won't affect my performance in the game.

But it isn't only when you are actually on the field that you can gain by concentrating on the match. Watching other players in action can teach you a lot – especially if you are prepared to talk to them and ask questions about what you see. You can never learn everything there is to know about cricket. It is a game full of surprises and there is always something new to discover.

I can spend hours talking to the other lads in my team, trying to see the game from their point of view. For instance, I try to learn from the spin bowlers at Somerset, Dennis Breakwell and Vic Marks. We talk about how they react to given situations, what they think their most dangerous delivery is, how to play it, all sorts of things.

Don't, however, be anxious to believe everything you are told. Cricket is full of theorists who can ruin your game in no time. But that doesn't mean you should never listen to people who are trying to help.

The old man who walks up to you and tells you what you are doing wrong may be an idiot – or he may have once been a Test player. You don't know. So listen to what he says, ask questions about it, decide for yourself what you can usefully try, and reject the rest. It is horribly easy to get brainwashed by theories and completely lost – I am sure it has happened to many promising young players. So develop the confidence to form your own opinions about what can help you.

On the subject of building confidence, a lot of

young players are frightened of a cricket ball. I have heard it said that they should start to play with a soft ball while they learn the game, and then progress on to a hard one. I am not sure I agree.

As a boy, if I ever had the choice between using a hard or soft ball, I plumped for the cricket ball. The sooner you get used to it, I believe, the better. It is hard, and of course it can hurt, but I think that is all the more reason to play with it as early as possible, because you soon grow used to it and become unafraid.

I can't remember being seriously hurt by a cricket ball, even as a boy. There is a simple principle to follow. Just as in football the lad who chickens out of a tackle at the last moment is the one who gets hurt, so too in cricket it is the one who is frightened of the ball who gets injured by it. If you attack the ball, smother it, get hold of it confidently in your hand, it won't hurt you. Ever. Back away nervously, stick out a tentative hand and withdraw it at the last moment, and you are going to get damaged and broken fingers. Just watch the ball all the way, and attack it.

Chapter 3 **Keep yourself fit**

To play cricket you have got to be fit. The character who turns out three stone overweight won't be making his contribution to the team. He may be physically heavy, but he is more than likely three stone light in the head.

Concentration, as I have said, is the most vital quality for a cricketer. And if you are tired and out of breath because you are not fit, you will not be able to concentrate hard for longer than an hour. Fatigue plays tricks with the mind and takes it away from the match.

I am sure professional cricketers are fitter now than they have ever been – just as I think fielding standards are also at an all-time high. The two are linked. Players field better because they are more mobile – and mentally they are more alert because they are fit.

The most basic requirement is stamina – the ability to keep going at your best all day. And that means a very high level of fitness. A footballer trains to run for ninety minutes – a cricketer has to train to be as fresh at six o'clock as he was when the day's play began.

There's no real substitute for running. Bob Willis runs five miles a day when he is not playing, and he gets the benefit when he can rip in with a devastating spell after tea in a Test match. It isn't unusual to find my Somerset team-mates, Keith Jennings and Hallam Moseley, out jogging around the County Ground in Taunton early in the morning on any day.

If you find distance running boring, and to be fair plenty of people do, then there are all sorts of ways to do the same job – playing five-a-side football, squash, badminton, swimming – anything which builds up your general level of fitness. If it is possible, add a competitive element to your training in some way. People tend to put far more effort in when competing.

You are the person who best knows when you are fit enough. You can kid yourself that you are better than you are, but the test is this. Can you concentrate for a two- or three-hour session in the field? Do you get out of breath quickly? Can you scramble that third run as quickly as you ran the first? If you lie in the answers to those questions, the only person you are cheating is yourself. It will be your results that suffer – you who drops catches, or gets run out.

There are four areas of the body which take extra strain if you are a bowler – the hamstrings, the groin muscles, the back and shoulders.

The hamstrings take an awful lot of strain, and ideally you should do some exercises to stretch them every day. I do this with the help of my Somerset team-mate, Peter Denning, who is a good foot shorter than I am. Quite simply I lift my foot up and rest it on his shoulder, with my leg straight. That stretches the hamstrings in my thighs and makes them more supple. I learnt this, incidentally, from Bob Willis, who does the same exercise before every England match with the England physiotherapist, Bernard Thomas.

If you haven't got the help of a friend, you can get the same effect by crossing your feet over and bending down to touch your toes with your legs straight.

Bowling puts terrific strain on the groin muscles, so it is important both to stretch them every day and to loosen them before you start a spell of bowling. The same routine does for both jobs.

You will see most professional bowlers doing this routine before they start a spell – and footballers before a game, too. Stand up straight with your legs apart, then put your weight on one leg which you flex at the knee. The other leg stays straight and you will feel the muscles inside it stretching.

The shoulders need to be loose and supple to make your action smooth – or to help you throw the ball swiftly when you are fielding. Exercises rolling them are the answer for this – swinging both arms around in a wide arc, or punching the air in front of your face. You can also stretch them by holding both hands together behind your head and pushing them sharply backwards.

A good quick bowler gets his back into the action to generate extra pace – Jeff Thomson is the best example. But you can't do that if your back muscles won't take it. Try these two routines. First, stand with your legs slightly apart, hands on hips, and twist your body, rolling it from the trunk. Then lie on your back with your legs crossed and try to touch each toe as far up the opposite leg as possible.

It sounds an arduous programme, but it only takes twenty or thirty minutes' running and five minutes of these exercises every day to put you in tip-top condition – and able to get the best from your natural talents for batting, bowling or fielding. If your mates take the 'micky' when they see you out pounding the streets, let them. You'll have the last laugh, because feeling fit is one of the greatest things in life.

Chapter 4 **The right equipment**

I hate to see an untidy cricketer. I am sure you know one, though. He turns up for matches with his boots all muddy and stained, as though he has just fished them out of a duckpond. His trousers are covered in grass stains, and creased because they have been screwed up in a ball in his kitbag since the last time he played, and he is wearing a thin nylon shirt with the buttons undone to get a sun tan. He looks untidy, and I am willing to bet his play is untidy as well.

Fifty per cent of cricket is confidence, believing in your own ability. You can give yourself confidence by being smart, feeling smart. If you look like a cricketer, rather than a tramp who happens to be wearing white clothes, you will feel like a cricketer. And if you feel like a cricketer, you are half-way to being one.

The Ian Botham of a few years ago didn't always come up to these standards himself, I must admit. But I learnt my lesson, for good, the hard way. During 1977, when I was first picked to play for England's Test team, I got very attached to a particular pair of boots. I decided they were my lucky boots and I insisted on wearing them long after they should have gone in the dustbin. The result? I injured my feet, and missed the final Test against the Australians because of it. Since then I have looked after all my equipment very carefully, and smartness has become something of a hobby-horse of mine.

Your boots are the most vital part of your equipment. They take the strain of running, keep you on your feet, and give your ankles support. Find a pair that are comfortable, and try not to be talked into getting some two sizes too big, because 'you'll grow into them'. You will grow into them, but you will also ruin your feet in the process. The boots should have a reasonably strong toe-cap, to give protection if you are hit on the foot, and if you bowl you will need adequate support around the heel and ankle. Buying boots with proper metal studs is the only way to be sure you will get a good firm grip if it is wet – and be prepared to spend the odd few pence every year on new studs, so that they are always long enough to do their job. I have seen people with perfect white boots, but nearly all the studs were missing or worn. That is silly. Look after your boots, and they will take care of you in return.

It is no good doing all the work to get fit to play cricket if you do something silly and injure yourself. Most of a cricketer's equipment is designed to protect and support the parts of the body which come under most strain. And that doesn't just apply to pads and gloves. A warm sweater, for instance, saves bowlers from just as many injuries as batting gloves do batsmen. If you do bowl then it is vital to keep your body warm after working up a sweat. If you let yourself get cold, you run the risk of pulling shoulder or back muscles if you have to return for a second spell. Even in Australia, on the hottest days of the tour with the temperature touching 100 degrees, I wore a sleeveless sweater after I had bowled. I didn't always wear it on to the field, but after bowling it was a must. In English weather it is even more essential. It may feel hot, but there is often a slight breeze, which is what can do the damage.

A clean pair of socks is equally important. I once had a foot complaint in Australia, caused by sweat, and it gave me a lot of pain. In England, where it isn't so hot, that shouldn't happen, providing you change your socks regularly. I like to wear two pairs, and put on fresh, clean ones for every session.

When you are batting, there are three essentials: pads, gloves and a box. That means both pads, incidentally. Nothing looks worse than a batsman with only his left leg padded – and what happens if the ball hits the other leg? I think fathers, schools, clubs, anybody with responsibility for teaching cricket to youngsters, should insist that they always wear the proper equipment. The right gear prevents you from being hurt and gives you confidence. I don't, however, think it is a good thing for schoolboys to wear helmets or thigh pads, or all the other protective paraphernalia. They can come later, as you progress into the higher classes of cricket.

I'm sorry if talking about clothing and clean socks is not as exciting as discussing hitting sixes or bowling bouncers, but it is very important, and if you get into good habits at an early stage you can avoid all sorts of problems later.

If you are lucky enough to be able to buy your own bat, it is worth knowing what to look for. You will be given all sorts of conflicting advice. Some people will say use a heavy bat – others will argue that a light one is better. Some will recommend a long handle, others will tell you to choose a short handle. At the shop there will probably be a salesman who wants you to take the most expensive one – and nearly all the different types will be autographed or recommended by famous Test cricketers.

Try to ignore all that. Forget it. It is your bat and you are the only person who knows what is best for you. And if someone wants to argue with you over your choice, then stick to your guns.

So what should you look for? The answer is you shouldn't look at all, but *feel*. Pick the bat up, and settle into your stance. Play a few imaginary shots. It should be heavy enough for you to control it, but light enough so that it is easy to lift back. It should feel balanced, and you should feel your stance is comfortable with it to know it is the right size. Feel that the balance is right, that you don't find it is top- or bottom-heavy. Pick through every bat in the shop, if need be, until you find the one that feels perfect to you. Don't be afraid to seem a nuisance and take your time over it. When you find the right bat, buy it and look after it carefully. It will repay you with runs.

Chapter 5 **Fielding**

I have never been able to understand people who moan about fielding. You hear them grumbling away, wishing they could bat or bowl, telling you they are bored. Well, I love fielding and so, I think, should any cricketer. And it is absolutely vital that it is done well.

That is why this chapter comes before batting or bowling. I decided to begin my book with the basics of the game, and fielding is the most basic part of all. It makes all the difference between winning and losing. A dropped catch can lose a match as surely as a century can win it. Good fielding has been a vital part of the present Somerset side – and even more so in the England team. I genuinely believe that there has never been a better England team in the field.

Yet in the past, fielding was looked on as a chore – and many county sides carried two or three people who weren't good enough. For some reason it took the limited-over competitions to wake people up to what they should have known for years.

Fielders put pressure on a batsman as much as any bowler. It's a great bonus for me when I am bowling for Somerset to know that I have Phil Slocombe's speed and accuracy on my side at cover. In the England team there are Derek Randall and David Gower doing the same job – making the batsmen terrified to take a run.

So the first message I want to get across is that if you think fielding is boring then it's entirely your fault because it isn't. There is no reason why you shouldn't be involved in some way with every ball. You start by concentrating, expecting the ball to come to you, and if it doesn't, you can back up the fielder it has gone to, or back up the wicket-keeper or bowler he is throwing to, even back up the man who is backing up. All those things save vital runs. There's an old adage: 'Every run you save is one less to score.' It is very true. The one-day competitions have emphasized it. If you let two fours go through your legs, and give away eight runs, you have possibly got to spend two overs batting to make them up again – and all completely unnecessary.

So let's start with the basics of stopping and throwing a ball. There are two ways to stop the ball – and in both cases the basic principle is to get your body behind it. Whenever you can, present the ball with a double barrier – two hands first and then your body. The most common way is to go down on one knee, so that you can provide a wide obstacle for the ball to hit if it suddenly changes direction off the ground. If you haven't got time to get there, the second way is to get both feet behind the ball, as shown in the other photograph.

How to throw the ball is very much an individual thing. The important thing is to get it as quickly as possible to the top of the stumps. And I stress that it should go to the *top* of the stumps. It is the easiest place to catch it. Nothing annoys a wicket-keeper more than having to take the ball on the half-volley – and it wastes vital seconds that could throw away a run-out chance.

Practice makes perfect. Every morning Phil Slocombe goes out and works for half an hour, with somebody hitting the ball to him, which he fields and throws back to the wicket-keeper.

There are times, when you are going for a run-out chance, when you will take the risk of not going down in either of the two stopping

Above: The best way to stop the ball – on one knee, making a wide obstacle

Right: Try to get your body behind both hands

SOMERSET
C.C.C.
NEXT

Two-handed pick-up and throw on the run. Attack the ball, head over it, keeping sideways-on, throwing hard to the top of the stumps

positions in order to throw the ball in more quickly. The picture sequences show you how it is done. Attack the ball, try to get there with two hands if you can, then send it whizzing back in. You'll see that as I pick the ball up and prepare to throw it, I am moving by crossing one leg behind the other. This keeps me balanced and sideways-on so that I can sight up the wicket I am throwing at. The pick-up and throw should be all one movement. You can practise it with a tennis ball against a brick wall. For extra speed you can pick the ball up with only one hand. In this case it is even more important to watch it all the way into your hand, and get your head over the ball as you field it.

The methods of throwing the ball vary a lot with each individual. Most people try to throw it in the same way you would throw a dart, and that is what most coaching books recommend. But the West Indian players tend to throw with an underarm sling, which is very powerful and accurate – and, in any case, you have to tailor it to how far you can throw with any particular method. The object is to get the ball in at a comfortable height quickly. Experiment to find the best way you can do that from different distances.

Incidentally, even if you specialize as a close-fielder you must still be able to do all this. There will be times when the circumstances of the game

A one-handed pick-up saves vital seconds

Watch the ball rather than the batsmen until you have safely picked it up

force you to field in the deep, and then if you can't stop and throw a ball you'll be a liability.

Every fielder should also practise taking high catches – the sort of difficult chance where the ball is hit high into the air, possibly spinning off the edge of the bat. You have to judge where it will fall, and move quickly to get under it. It is sometimes tempting to run towards it before you know where it will land, but the problem then is that it is hard to move back if you have misjudged it and it is dropping over your head. Give yourself a split-second to judge it and then move into position quickly.

There are two different techniques of catching the high ball. Choose which suits you best. The orthodox method is to take it with your hands together, linked by your little fingers, in front of your eyes, and then let the hands ride down to your chest with the ball. I personally prefer a different method, which I learnt in Australia, and which you can see in the photographs overleaf. Hold the hands with the thumbs together, again catching the ball at eye level, and this time let the hands give into the shoulders. In either case, providing you let your hands give with the impact of the ball, it will never hurt you.

My specialist fielding position is second slip. It isn't an easy job and it has taken me years of practice to master it. I still have to practise hard to keep sharp.

CATCHING A SKIER A eyes on the ball

B hands together

C let the hands give with the ball

The secret of slip fielding is to find a comfortable stance, low down, with your hands touching, or just above the gound. Concentration is especially important, because you can go long periods without touching the ball – but when the chance does come you have only got a split-second to judge it. Stay down low until you read the height the catch will be. On English wickets, which don't give much bounce, most slip catches will come low, and it is easier to get up quickly than it is to go back down. I should think a very high percentage of the catches I have dropped have been because I stood up too soon.

Close-fielders are the one set of people who break the rule of watching the ball all the time. At first slip you can watch the ball all the way from the bowler, but at second slip and all the other close-catching positions it is easier to concentrate on the edge of the bat. That is where a chance will come from – and you learn to anticipate the shot which is coming.

Gully is a difficult position at which to field. The ball will often come to you from a full-blooded shot, which means your reflexes have to be very fast. And another position which calls for quick reflexes is the 'bat pad' position, forward short leg. I always wear a helmet to field there – especially after one saved my life during the Fourth Test at Sydney in 1979. Rick Darling pulled a short ball savagely and it hit me on the temple before I could get out of the way. Without a helmet I am sure I would have been killed. In club and school cricket, when you haven't got the protection of a helmet, learn to anticipate the shot and curl yourself into a tight ball to protect yourself against an obvious attacking shot. One more thing – you may not have a helmet available – but always wear a box.

There has been a lot of criticism of fielders wearing helmets. People say it gives the fielder an unfair advantage. I believe that's nonsense, and think people who say it must never have fielded close to the bat. You don't go any closer with the helmet on, all you do is give yourself protection. It is a very dangerous position to field – and, incidentally, if you are a bowler respect the man who is doing the job for you. He has shown confidence in your bowling to field that close – so don't send down a lot of rubbish which invites a hefty blow to leg.

The best way to practise close-catching is with some friends. One has the bat, and one is the thrower. The rest fan out in the slip positions as they would for a match. The thrower aims for the bat, and the batter nicks it towards the slips – which gives you the same sort of chances you'll get in a match. I find that much better than simply throwing the ball at somebody with a bat and him patting it back to you. But again, it's a matter of individual choice. Phil Edmonds, who is a very good close-catcher, likes to have somebody hitting the ball at him. If you have to practise on your own, it's back to the brick wall and tennis ball, sharpening your reactions by standing as close to the wall as possible to take the rebounding ball.

I'd like to end this chapter by emphasizing two golden rules of fielding.

1 Two hands are always better than one – and safer still with the body behind them.

2 Concentrate, and get involved.

Do this and you'll find that fielding is the most enjoyable part of the game.

Chapter 6 **Batting**

For a batsman, there are six golden rules.

1 Concentrate.
2 Keep your head still and get it over the ball.
3 Get behind the line.
4 Get your foot to the pitch of the ball when you play forward.
5 Bring the bat through straight.
6 Extend the arms when you play shots.

These are six qualities which make up a good batsman. Watch any successful county or Test player and you will see him obeying all these rules – no matter what else may be wrong according to the traditional text-books. If things are not going well for you, it is probably because you are doing one of these basic things wrong. When these are correct you can safely play all sorts of unusual shots. Without them you can never guarantee success.

Let me take them one by one. I have already said a lot about concentration. I will just add that most people can bat for as long as they can concentrate. When their mind begins to wander they are far more likely to be out. This is the quality which separates people who make fifty from those who score centuries.

Keeping your head still is very important – and is probably the rule that club and school players break most often. If your head is bobbing all over the place you lose your bearings and judgement. You can't be sure where your stumps are, or how high or low the ball is bouncing, or how fully or short it is pitched. It provides an anchor for all the other movements, keeping control on everything you do. Watch Viv Richards for the perfect example of how to do this. Even when he is being aggressive, chasing runs, inventing shots to force away accurate bowling, his head remains still and his eyes are on the ball. Indeed, it is the only way anybody can be consistently successful in this.

It is equally important to get your head over the ball as you hit it. This gives you complete control. The ball cannot do anything to surprise you, because you know where it is. You have mastered it. This is especially important when playing back, and is, in any case, the thing which ensures you don't hit the ball into the air.

Getting into line with the ball means that you reduce your margin of error. A bat is only 4¼ inches wide, and you want to hit the ball in the middle of that. If you don't move your feet so that you are behind the line, you will find yourself being caught behind and in the slips from edges, or bowled between your bat and pad.

To make sure you are in line, get your foot alongside the pitch of the ball when you play forward. It also gives you balance and the control to keep the ball down when you hit it – which should normally be your aim. It will, incidentally, mean that your head will almost automatically be over the ball as you make contact.

One of the first things any boy is told when he takes up the game is 'keep a straight bat'. In many cases, it is something which he doesn't understand and never masters. For a start, it sounds silly. A bat is straight, and the only way to bend it is over your knee, and then it is likely to snap! So what does it mean? Well, if you draw a line on the pitch directly underneath the path of the ball, your bat should move vertically along that line as you swing it. It's as simple as that.

Again this is all to do with reducing the margin of error. If you swing across that line there is only one split-second when your bat can hit the ball. It could bounce over or under the blade, or on to the edge. But if your bat goes vertically along the line it *must* come into contact with the ball at some stage. At first this is difficult to do, because it is natural to swing across the line. The secret is to let the top hand do all the work. That is the hand which must control the bat, with the bottom hand adding power. The way to master this is to practise playing shots with only your left hand holding the bat. That develops the strength you need to play correctly.

When you are settled in your stance your arms will both be slightly bent at the elbow. As you begin the backswing, lifting the bat up as the bowler's arm comes over, they will bend further – but at the moment you hit the ball they must be straight. It is the extension of your arms into that position which gives you timing and power to stroke the ball away past the fielders – so aim never to hit the ball with the arms bent. The power should come from the arms and shoulders rather than the wrists. Too much wrist movement and you will tend to spoon the ball into the air.

So these are all the qualities you must have. They are attributes possessed by all top players. Other aspects of batting, I believe, are more open to the individual to develop his own style. That includes even simple things like grip and stance.

The grip of the bat is straightforward. For a beginner the easiest way to find it is to lay it face down, and then pick it up as if it were an axe and you were going to raise it over your head to chop a piece of wood. If you still have doubts, take a look at the photograph of my grip. You will see my hands are together, and near to the top of the bat. That is the way I would recommend, but again, providing you don't break the six golden rules, you may hold it a different way. Asif Iqbal of Kent, the Pakistan captain, has his hands a long way apart on the handle. In theory he shouldn't be able to drive fluidly like that – but it doesn't seem to stop him. The test, as ever, is whether your unorthodox grip inhibits your batting in any way.

The stance is open to even more individual approaches. My own is fairly orthodox and would be reasonable for a beginner to copy. You can see it in the photograph. But there are hundreds of different stances and you may find you develop your own. Again, ask yourself the question, am I doing the basics right? Then stand in the most comfortable way. Ken Barrington's stance was very open, meaning his chest faced down the wicket, which certainly isn't the way traditional text-books advise. It didn't stop him scoring runs though. As a complete contrast, Peter Roebuck of Somerset stands almost like a hunchback. It looks hideously uncomfortable to me – yet it is just right for him. If you are comfortable, and are doing the basics right, you have found the stance that suits you. Don't change unless it is for a good reason. You might find the classic text-book stance which you are told to adopt feels cramped and uncomfortable.

In the photo-sequences later on you will find that every shot begins with me lifting my bat as the bowler's arm comes over. Again, traditionally, it is said the backlift should take the bat above the stumps. You will see that mine does not – I take it out to about third slip. The important thing is that when it comes through to meet the ball it is straight. Apply that test to your own backlift. You may find that lifting it back straight helps you to bring it down straight – or you may feel more comfortable with a similar backlift to my own. It is your choice, providing the final result is the same – a straight bat.

I am sure that one of the things which confuses most school or club players is taking guard. It is a subject which attracts all sorts of theories. I think there would be less confusion if it was realized *why* you take guard. The object is simple. You need to know where your off-stump is, to help you judge when to leave the ball. By always standing in the same place, you keep your bearings constant and develop an instinct for the ball that is wide. If you have got that quality you can leave alone a ball which is six inches wide, and let it pass harmlessly to the wicket-keeper. If you don't know that it is wide, you have to play at it.

As a bowler I can see the people who don't know where their stumps are, and they are a delight to bowl at. They turn bad balls into good ones by playing at deliveries they should leave

The grip

The stance

alone. I can draw them out and get them caught at slip or by the wicket-keeper. A good player just lets the ball whistle past when he is on the defensive. One of the best leavers of the ball I have played against was the Australian, Greg Chappell. He knew where his stumps were, and if he was trying to consolidate, he was terribly frustrating to bowl at. It wasn't only his off-stump that he knew the position of – anything that was wide of leg-stump got brutally punished.

The guard, then, helps you develop this vital instinct. You can stand and look at the stumps, and think you know where they are – yet when you are settled into your stance and concentrating on the ball in the bowler's hand, it isn't so easy, because, of course, you are looking the other way.

The three most common guards are leg-stump, middle and leg, and middle. The only way to decide which suits you best is to try each of them, and see which gives you the best feel of where your stumps are. Nobody can tell you to take a particular guard – you have to develop the instinct for it from wherever you are happiest. I find middle and leg suits me best, and I always use it. Other players change their guard for different types of bowling, or when they are attacking or defending. Again, that is their choice. The important thing is to know why you are taking a particular guard – and not to just chop and change because somebody else does.

If you have mastered the business of playing shots and found a comfortable guard, there is still one quality you need in order to become an accomplished batsman: the ability to build an innings.

It is a process which should begin from the time you get padded up, before you even go out to bat. You can watch the game closely while you are waiting to go in, and get an idea of what the bowlers are doing. Are they making it swing or turn? How fast or slow are they? Where are the gaps in the field?

When you walk out to the middle take this opportunity to get used to the light. Look up at the sky, look around the field. Personally, I like to throw the bat around with each arm like a windmill a couple of times. It gets my shoulders warmed up – and it is also partly a psychological thing. It helps make me feel prepared.

At the wicket take a good look to see if the field has changed and take guard. Have a walk up the wicket to find out if there are any awkward looking patches. Then, only when you are ready, settle down to face your first ball. Don't rush – unless, of course, you are in a situation where every second is vital because you are chasing quick runs. The most dangerous delivery you will face is the very first because normally you aren't used to the pitch, the pace of the bowler or the light. So don't face it until you are ready, even if it takes you a minute or so to settle down.

Don't be frightened to ask the batsman at the other end questions. He has been there for a while facing up to the bowling and knows what is going on. He can tell you to watch for a quicker ball, or if there is turn or swing, or whether the ball is cutting off the seam. Use his knowledge to give yourself a head start, rather than waiting to find it all out for yourself.

Take the first few overs easily, making survival your principal aim. Then, as you begin to settle in, you can start looking to score runs. Try to treat each ball as it comes, though. A long hop is a long hop whether you have only just come in or have already scored a century. It deserves to go for four. Throughout the innings it is vital to treat each ball on its merits. Never make up your mind to play a particular shot before the ball is bowled.

The most priceless asset you can develop as a batsman is timing. If you can hit the ball just at the perfect moment you will never need to hit it hard. Clive Lloyd and Viv Richards are examples of players who seem to stroke fours and sixes. The best I have ever seen was Colin Cowdrey. He seemed to play a forward defensive, yet, because his timing was so good, the ball would be racing through the covers for four.

That is a quality which comes only with practice. In fact, the only way to become a good batsman is by batting regularly – you certainly won't improve by just talking about it, or even by reading this book. You have to take the advice on to the field, and put it into practice. Take every chance you can to get out and play – even if it is only in the backyard with one friend and a tennis ball. The more practice you get the more you will improve.

In a match, as I said earlier, it is vital that you fit in as part of a team – making your contribution towards the overall success. That makes it essential to run well between the wickets. Nobody will like a team-mate who scores fifty but runs four people out.

Everything depends on calling. Only use three calls; 'yes', when you believe you can both safely run; 'no', when you don't think you can; 'wait' when you aren't sure but think there could be a chance. You and your partner must trust each other's judgement at all times. You have responsibility for his safety, he for yours. When you judge a run decide whether you can both make it safely. When the ball goes in front of the batsman it is his call, when it goes behind him it is the non-striker's responsibility. Follow that and you should never have any problems.

You can make taking runs easier by backing up. That means taking a pace or two down the wicket in anticipation of a run when you are the non-striker. In tight finishes I have seen people successfully take a run to the wicket-keeper, simply because the non-striker was already half-way down the wicket when the batsman played his shot. In any case, aim to run the first one quickly. It puts pressure on the fielders, and will often turn singles into twos.

When you bat with somebody regularly an understanding develops between you. For instance the Somerset opening batsmen, Brian Rose and Pete Denning, often don't give a shout for the run. They have batted together almost every day for three seasons, and they know when to go and when not to. Outside the professional game it is harder to build that sort of relationship – so it is always safer to call. And call loud. It is no use muttering 'no' so quietly that your partner is half-way down the wicket before he realizes you have sent him back. Leave him in no doubt.

You will never be a perfect batsman – but with hard work you can become very good. Be prepared to watch and learn from people who are better players than you – and that means going to some county and Test matches. As a boy I always tried to watch the best batsmen and learn from them. I still do it even now.

My boyhood heroes were Gary Sobers and Ken Barrington. Ken, who has been an England selector and tour manager since he retired with 6,806 Test runs to his credit, could concentrate for as long as anybody I have seen. It didn't worry him if he spent two hours without making a run. He was still there, and eventually he would get on top.

Gary Sobers, now deservedly Sir Gary Sobers, had the ability to dominate bowlers. He was still playing for Nottinghamshire when I first appeared for Somerset, and I remember looking on him with awe. For me, his quality was summed up in a John Player League match. I beat him outside the off-stump with the first ball I bowled. I felt marvellous – until he sent the next one whistling back over my head for four. I don't think any bowler could claim to have dominated him.

The man I love to watch and learn from now, and whom I consider the best in the world, is my Somerset team-mate, Viv Richards. We began the game together and I have watched him develop, just, I suppose, as he has watched me. He is a great friend – but beyond that he is a great player. His technique is almost perfect, but he combines that with flair. He plays some unorthodox shots when he is chasing runs, but even then he gets the basics right. His timing is magnificent, and it sometimes amazes me to see him hit the ball so hard with so little effort. He makes the game look so easy – and if you want somebody to learn from there's nobody better.

Chapter 7 The principal shots

In the previous chapter I ran through the basics of batting – the golden rules to take to the crease. These should be the basis of your batting style.

I don't, however, think it is sensible for a beginner to try unorthodox methods too quickly. Keeping to the classic 'text-book' shots at first will help you master the basics before you try to launch out. In this chapter I am going to show them to you.

I will try not to get bogged down in details of the mechanics of playing them. The pictures should show where the feet move to, where the body weight goes and how the ball is struck. Instead, I am going to concentrate on when to use a particular shot, the danger points to watch for and common faults to avoid. Reading the text and studying the pictures will give you the main principles. Take what you learn and practise it.

The forward defensive

You will not score runs off every ball you receive. Sometimes you will be forced to defend, and the forward defensive is the main shot you will use to do so. It is played to a good length, straight ball – anything in that nasty area where you are not sure whether to play forward or back. It is always best then to go forward and smother the ball with a dead bat.

The essential elements of the shot are getting the bat and pad together, your head over the ball, and playing with a controlled, dead bat.

You can see from the photographs how the shot is played. As I judge the length of the delivery, and know I must play a forward defensive, I begin to lean into the ball, bringing my bat down from the backswing. That means I am throwing my weight forward, my body goes first and my foot automatically follows. The heel of my front foot acts as a pivot as I land on it, and then the rest of my foot slams down, taking the weight with it. By throwing the body forward in this way I ensure that my head is over the ball.

You will see that although my backlift goes towards third slip, the bat actually plays the shot perfectly straight. This is because I controlled it with my left hand. If I let the right hand come in, I would hit across the line and wouldn't be sure to connect. The top hand is the control, the bottom supplies power – and for a defensive shot you don't need power. The angle of the bat when I make contact with the ball kills it. The blade is facing downwards, and that is where the ball goes, giving no chance of a catch to any close fielders. The aim is to completely smother the ball.

I have used words like 'throwing' weight and 'slamming' the foot down to give an idea that this all has to be done quickly – especially against genuinely fast bowlers, obviously. But it should be a controlled movement, with the head remaining still, so that your judgement of line is not lost – essential if you are to see whether the ball is swinging late or turning.

When you have judged the line of the ball, move your front foot to land just inside it, with the bat following down the line. The two should be close together to present an impenetrable barrier – never leave a 'gate' between them for the ball to go through.

If you can play a good, solid, forward defensive shot you have got the cement with

THE FORWARD DEFENSIVE A foot to the pitch of the ball

B head over the ball, straight bat

C bat and pad are close together

which to build an innings. It holds you together when you are facing a particularly awkward spell of bowling. Occupying the crease is an essential part of batting – you cannot score runs if you are back in the pavilion.

The backward defensive

When the ball has pitched on a shorter length, it isn't easy to get forward and smother it because it bounces too high. The answer then is to go back and smother it. That is the essence of the backward defensive shot.

Again, follow the golden rules. Concentrate, keep your head still, get behind the line, get your head over the ball, bring the bat through straight.

The biggest danger in playing this shot is not getting behind the line. It is horribly easy to find yourself just dangling the bat out like washing in the wind – which is asking to be caught behind or in the slips.

The photographs show how I solve the problem. My back foot moves across and right behind the line of the ball. In that position I can see if it swings away late, and take the bat away if I want to. Many people get into trouble by pushing the ball out to point or gully instead of hitting through the ball. That is a cardinal error. I am not saying you will never be beaten by a ball that swings away very late – you have got to give the bowler some credit, after all. But getting your back foot across and behind the line, and playing with a good straight bat, gives him far less chance.

Against very fast bowling I move my foot back and across as the bowler's arm comes over. I find it gives me more time to see the ball and judge the line and length. When you play forward it is very difficult to get back – but if you start by going back it is very easy to change and go forward instead. In any case, against very fast bowling you will tend to play more off the back foot.

THE BACKWARD DEFENSIVE
A below: moving back and across

B above right: getting behind the line
C below right: dead straight bat

Schweppes

D still watching the ball

The classic coaching theory is that you should remain still until you begin to play the shot. I think that is a good theory – but in practice, for me, it doesn't work. I have played against some of the quickest bowlers in the world – and I don't think I could have survived by remaining completely still.

Now I am not saying you should be jumping around like a cat on hot bricks. The movement, like every movement you make while you are batting, must be controlled and your head must remain still. You will see in the pictures that my head stays still throughout the shot. Providing I do that, it is quite safe to move back and across to prepare to face a fast bowler. I have talked to most of today's top players about this, and they nearly all favour going back and across. This isn't a recent development, no matter what some people might have you believe. I have watched films of older players. Ken Barrington, for example, went back and across against fast bowling.

I have said a lot about attacking, and enjoying hitting the ball and scoring runs. Yet, when I started discussing the individual shots, I began with two that were defensive. Why? Because, if you cannot keep out the good balls, you will not be there to play aggressive shots against the bad balls.

The cover-drive

Watching anybody score runs is exciting – but seeing a good batsman cover-drive is one of the finest sights in the game. It is a shot played with power but also grace and control. Moreover, it is perfectly safe, because the ball whizzes along the ground.

The shot is played to a ball which is overpitched, so that you can get forward, throwing your weight just as you did for the forward defensive, but instead, meeting the ball on the half-volley and letting the bat flow through

THE COVER-DRIVE A above: backlift B below: foot tc the pitch

C **head over the ball**
D **extending the arms**

the shot. If I am bowling and I send down a half-volley I get annoyed with myself, because on any type of wicket it is a wasted ball. I sometimes fall into the trap when the ball is swinging, because I then bowl a fuller length to try to get extra swing. It is rare to see top bowlers helping the batsmen with such a gift delivery. Rodney Hogg probably bowled only one or two in a whole winter in Australia – and I think Mike Hendrick last bowled one in about 1969!

It is extending the arm which turns a forward defensive into a flowing cover-drive. As you start to go forward you begin to see the ball is overpitched, and simply let the bat flow right through the shot. To get most power your arms should be straight at the moment of impact – and if you do that correctly the follow-through will come almost automatically.

Timing is all-important here. It isn't a power shot in the sense that, in theory, you should be able to play it without your bottom hand on the bat. In fact, when I injured my wrist before going to Australia in 1978, I built the strength back up by playing cover-drives with only my left hand. I took half a dozen cricket balls into the nets, and practised by dropping a ball with my right hand, and just extending the left arm on its own to stroke the ball away. This is an excellent exercise for building up strength and control in your left arm. If you are right-handed it may not be very strong, so five minutes a day like this will help correct that. I have been told that Sir Don Bradman used to practise like this with a stump and a golf ball. He used the stump as a bat and would stroke the golf ball away with it. That was possibly why he scored so many runs.

To keep the ball on the ground, make sure you get the basics right – your head over the ball, body in line, your foot to the pitch and a straight bat. There are few finer feelings for a batsman than hitting a cover-drive perfectly, watching the ball skim away across the outfield for four.

The on-drive

You don't see this shot in many coaching books – presumably because it is so similar to the cover-drive. But I have included it because there is an added complication which makes it a more difficult shot to play.

Quite simply it is this. When you are cover-driving it is comparatively easy to play down the line, because you are sending the ball back to roughly where it came from. When you on-drive there is a tendency to try to hit across the line.

The most common reason for this error is attempting to hit the ball in front of the pad. If you do that, you give yourself no chance, because your bat has to go across the line.

If you look closely at the photographs (overleaf) of this shot, and the cover-drive, you might spot the important difference. It is the position of my front foot. In the cover-drive my toes point towards mid-off, whereas in the on-drive I have opened my foot out, and given myself more room to play the shot. That is really all there is to it – give yourself room and let the arms extend.

An on-drive is not an easy shot to play. If you don't open out and give yourself enough room it is easy to overbalance – your head will move and you will lose sight of the ball. If you get stumped trying to on-drive it is probably because you don't make enough room for yourself to play the shot.

I think it is a good rule never to try to hit the ball too hard when you are on-driving. Timing is quite sufficient, and a lusty swipe at the ball is more likely to make you lose your balance. Again Colin Cowdrey was the all-time great at this. He stroked the bat through the shot, and you would expect him to get a single. In fact, he had timed it so well that the ball had sped for four.

A sure sign that you are not opening your front foot out enough is if you are hitting your toes or pad with the inside edge of the bat. Try to get your toes facing more towards mid-on. One important point: giving yourself room doesn't mean your front foot isn't at the pitch of the ball. If it isn't in the right place you will not get your head over the ball, and that is when you are likely to hit the ball in the air.

Driving off the back foot

There is a lot of psychology in cricket. Bowlers and opposing captains will try to exploit your nerves and put you under pressure while you are

THE ON-DRIVE A left: giving myself room to play the shot

B below: head over the ball

C above right: extending the arms
D below right: follow-through

hweppes

batting. Against a quick, accurate bowler the chances are that he will do it by putting a ring of slips and gullies behind you.

Because you are being attacked, it is a natural reaction to defend, to play safe and forget about scoring runs for a while. That only puts even more pressure on you. Before long you will be worried both because you are under attack and because you are not scoring runs.

The answer is to counter by taking quick singles. It keeps the scoreboard ticking, keeps your confidence high and puts pressure back on the opposition. They have to decide whether to keep their attacking field, or stop you from taking runs.

A drive off the back foot is one of the most useful shots for this purpose. When you are under attack, and perhaps there is no mid-off, you can use it to push the ball back and run for a single. I wouldn't, however, advise trying to hit it hard, as I have done in these pictures, until you are settled in and can judge the pace of the ball.

DRIVING OFF THE BACK FOOT A above: back and across

B above: full backlift

C below: weight all on back foot

D follow-through

The shot is similar to the backward defensive – except that you are scoring from a ball to which you would have defended early in your innings. Get behind the line and over the ball, but instead of playing with a dead bat let your arms flow through the shot. You are pushing at the ball and, as I said when talking about the backward defensive, that can be dangerous. So make sure you have been there long enough to judge the pace of the ball off the wicket, and whether there is any swing, or if the ball is cutting from the seam. If it is moving, think very carefully before you play this shot.

The important thing is to get over the ball. If you are hitting it on the top of the bat you cannot get any control or power, so it is best merely to defend. But if the bounce is not so high that is the time to hit the ball hard.

The cut

The cut, the hook and the sweep are three of cricket's most spectacular shots. But they also force you to break one of the six golden rules in playing them. In every other shot you are bringing the bat through straight, at right angles to the ground. With these three your bat is parallel to the ground.

That makes it vital you know the pace of the wicket and are seeing the ball well. In other words think twice about playing any of these shots early in your innings.

That word of caution over, the cut is a favourite shot of mine. Play it right and you send the ball fizzing away with enormous power. It should be played to a wide ball which pitches short of a length outside off-stump, a bad ball,

THE CUT A above: back and across B below: weight moving to the back foot

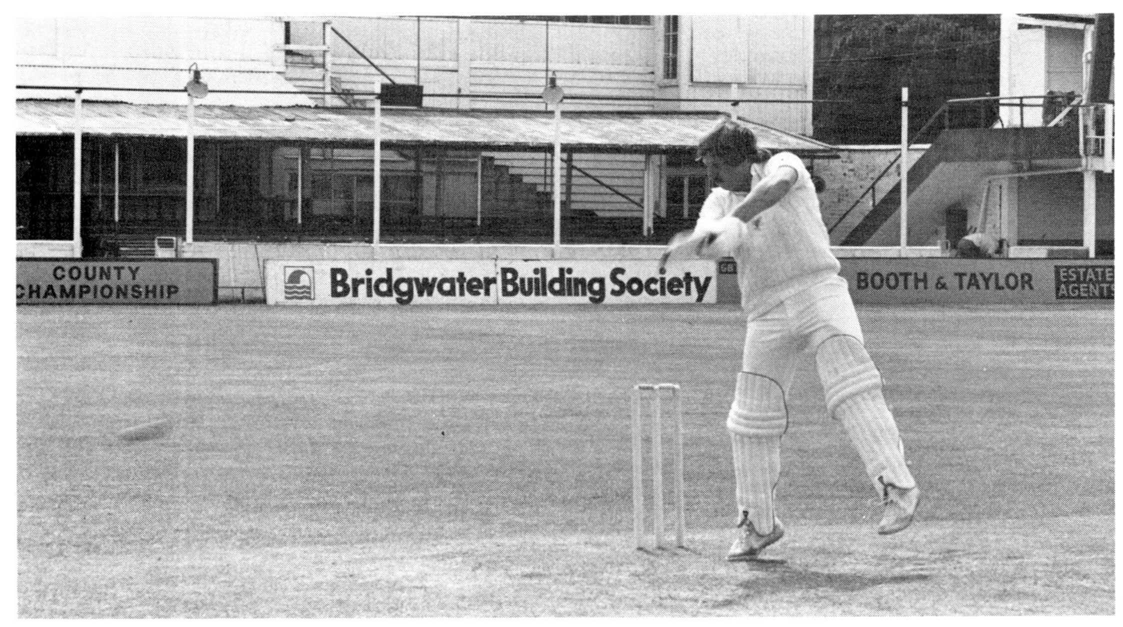

COUNTY
CHAMPIONSHIP
Bridgwater Building Society
BOOTH & TAYLOR
ESTATE
AGENTS

UNTY
PIONSHIP
Bridgwater Building Society
BOOTH & TAYLOR
ESTATE
AGENTS
SMIT

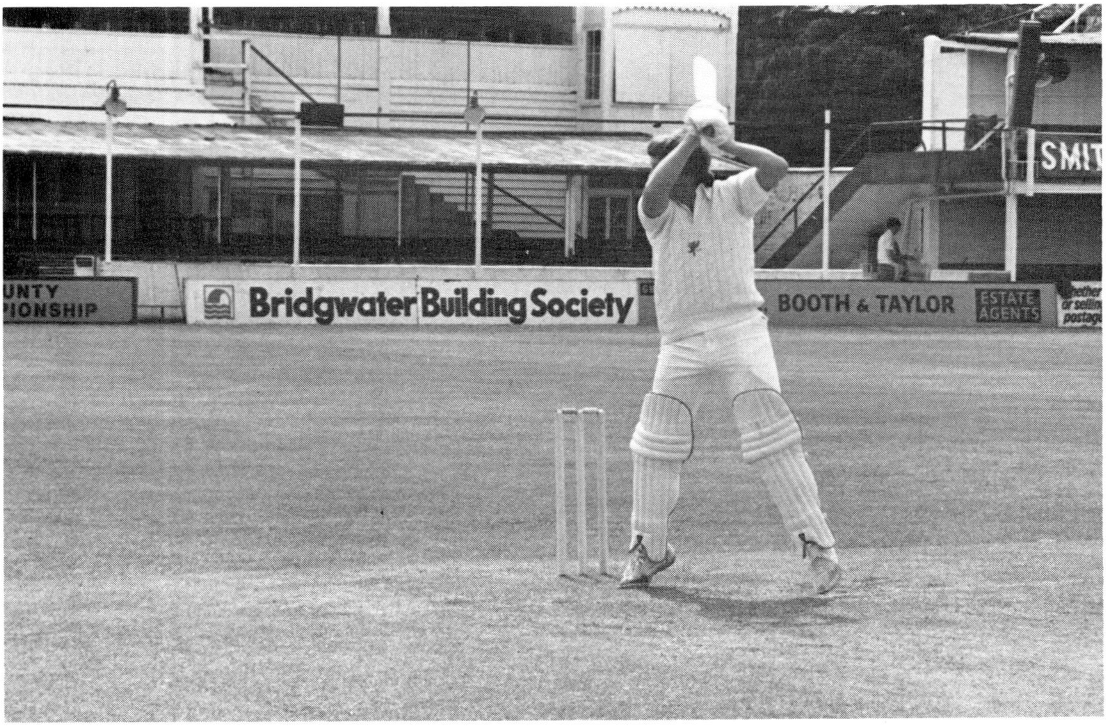

C above left: arms extended, wrists rolled . . . the ball is going down D below left: follow-through

which is begging to be hit. If I get cut when I am bowling I get very annoyed, because it really is a poor ball.

Be careful about trying to cut the ball if it is fairly straight. To get real power on it you want to play it with the arms fully extended – if the ball is too straight you will not be able to do that. You will find yourself straining, completely tucked up, and having to move out of line to get the bat there. That ball is best left alone.

The sequence of photographs shows how I played the shot. As I picked up the length and flight of the ball I put my weight on to my back foot, keeping my head still, and leant into the ball as I extended my arms out square to hit it. Against a fast bowler it is not necessary to hit it too hard, because the speed of the ball will do most of the work. But otherwise it is basically a right-hand power shot. Your top hand guides the bat into position and the bottom hand hits the ball hard.

Roll the wrists over the ball to keep it down. You must aim to hit it into the ground first, because otherwise you risk giving a simple catch to gully or point.

If you want somebody to watch, then Gordon Greenidge, Hampshire's West Indian opening batsman, is probably the most vicious cutter of a ball I have seen.

The hook

If it is exciting to watch somebody cut, then the hook is probably the most breathtaking shot of all. It is played against a bouncer, a ball that is a bit short and rears high towards your head. When a bowler tries to give you a 'bumper' he is laying down a challenge. Hooking him for four or six is the perfect answer.

In many ways it is probably the most aggressive stroke in cricket. It shows you are not scared of anything the bowler has to offer. That is really why I think it is a shame that the rules were altered to allow only one bouncer an over. If I have just hooked somebody for four I would like to do it again the next ball. And imagine telling a bowler who had just been mercilessly hooked by Viv Richards not to bowl another bouncer – that is probably the last thing he would want to try. I think it is sad that some of the spectacle might be taken out of the game.

Viv, incidentally, is probably the most vicious hooker in the game. I am glad I usually only bowl to him in the nets! In many ways it is not surprising that he and other West Indies players hook better than most, because it is a shot which requires true, hard wickets with an even bounce. Like the cut, it is a cross-batted shot, and so it is not one to be attempted in English conditions until you have got your eye in and are reading the bounce well. You have got to hit the ball at the perfect height – a top or bottom edge is probably going to give the wicket-keeper a simple catch.

The basic mistakes to avoid are not getting in line and taking your eye off the ball. You will sometimes see people going for the hook when they are not behind the line – but if they miss the ball they are the people who will get hurt. If you get behind it you can see any late movement clearly, and the instinct of self-preservation will automatically bring your head out of the way, letting the ball go through safely. In fact, you can see from the pictures that my body has swung right across and outside the line, which is best of all.

Taking your eye off the ball is always a mistake which can get you out. When you are hooking, it is a mistake which can get you badly hurt. Look at the photographs and you will see that I hit the ball in front of my face. At the moment of contact I was looking along the blade of the bat at the ball. That meant I was in complete control. Yet so many people tend to turn their head out of the way at that crucial moment. They would have no chance if they got an edge – and, in any case, turning the head and shutting the eyes makes it more likely they would get an edge. It goes back to the maxim that the person who gets hurt by the ball is the one who is afraid of it. For some it is an instinctive reaction to twist their head away. But if you are like that you must train yourself to keep your eyes on the ball and your head still all the time. The first principle of cricket is 'eyes on the ball'.

The shot should be played with the arms

THE HOOK A above left: into position

B right: head watching the ball – it is vital to get behind the line

extended, and, like the cut, the wrists rolled to avoid the danger of being caught. To try to explain the principle of extending your arms in this case, stand in your stance and, looking at the bowler all the time, throw a ball as hard as you can towards the square-leg umpire. You will release the ball in front of you, with your arm straight. That is exactly what your arm does when you play the hook, but obviously holding the bat.

A word of caution: before you play the hook, or any other shot, think about the field placings. I remember bowling against Gloucestershire for Somerset, and Zaheer Abbas, who loves to hook, was batting. We set a trap for him, with a man three-quarters of the way back behind square leg

C wrists rolled to keep the ball down safely

– and the first time I fed him with a bouncer he hit it straight down the fielder's throat for a simple catch. He ought to have seen the trap and geared himself not to be tempted into it.

Incidentally, in the second innings of that match we got him out again in the same way – but only after he scored a century. That brings me to another point. What Zaheer probably did was calculate the risks. He divided the number of runs he scores through hooking by the number of times it gets him out, and decided it brought him enough runs to gamble on playing it. If you stopped playing every shot you got out to, you would end up not playing any shots at all.

I have probably been out playing every shot in the book and a few more – but I would hate to think that would stop me playing attacking strokes. If you want to score runs, you have got to be prepared to attack. The important thing is to calculate the risks involved, decide which are acceptable and take them, and which are too dangerous and cut them out.

The sweep

The sweep is just the sort of shot which will send you racing to a calculator to work out the risk. A lot of people will tell you not to play it, and a great many coaching books ignore it and pretend it doesn't exist. I think that's a pity because it is a fine shot which can bring a lot of runs.

Play it against an off-spinner, where the ball is turning into you, to any delivery that is slightly over-pitched and on your leg stump or outside. Do not be tempted into trying it against any bowler who is turning the ball to the off, because that is asking to get top edges.

The essence is control. Don't try to whack the ball out of the ground. Just get your head over the ball, go down into a crouched position, with your front foot getting to the pitch of the ball, and roll the wrists to steer it safely along the ground. You can use the pace of the bowler to help it on its way, and should aim to steer it into the gaps in the field.

I am not pretending it is a particularly easy shot. In fact, during the 1978 Test series against New Zealand I got out trying to play it in both the first two Tests. I decided I must be doing something wrong and when, in the Third Test, Stephen Boock kept feeding me the ball to sweep I resisted the temptation. By the time Somerset played Sussex in the Gillette Cup Final, however, I had worked on the shot in the nets, and I used it against their spinners and scored a lot of runs.

I do not think I have seen anybody play it better than Alan Knott, the Kent and former England wicket-keeper. He must have scored an enormous number of runs with it over the years. He is an example of the sort of thinking I have tried to get over in my chapters on batting. 'Knotty' is an immensely unorthodox batsman, he must give the purists nightmares. But he gets all the basics right while he is improvising. It might annoy the critics, but it upsets bowlers even more. Bowling to an orthodox batsman is comparatively easy. You know where he is likely to hit any given delivery, you can test him and set the field accordingly. Trying to set a field to someone like Alan Knott is a real headache. You never know where he might hit the ball.

The lofted drive

I have said a lot about being confident and aggressive, so when I say this is another shot that requires caution it probably sounds as if I am contradicting myself. Yet the object of the game must always be *controlled* aggression. If you are attacking in a blind rage you become an easy prey for a good bowler – and you will soon be in a blind rage with yourself back in the pavilion.

This is the one shot which you deliberately hit into the air. Every other shot in this book is played with the intention of keeping the ball down. So before you go dashing down the wicket and heaving the ball to the heavens, you have got to ask yourself two things. First, are the fielders set back in a position to catch me? Second, am I strong enough to lift it over them? If you answer yes to the first and no to the second then forget this shot for the time being. And remember that if you are under thirteen or fourteen years old, it is unlikely that you will have the strength to clear a fielder on the boundary. You must be honest with yourself. If you are not, you will be found out.

If you don't think you can clear the fielder, then frankly you have to be an idiot to play this shot.

I think it is best to reserve the 'charge' down the wicket for times when the field is reasonably close, and for playing a spinner. Running down the wicket against a fast bowler is normally a sign of nerves.

I normally employ the lofted drive as a device to move the field back – leaving a nice big space into which you can push the ball for a single. We call that 'milking' the bowler, continually taking easy runs. I remember that when I scored my first century for Somerset, on a beautiful wicket at Trent Bridge against Nottinghamshire in 1976, we did just that. I reached fifty very quickly, hitting the ball over the close field – and then took

THE SWEEP A on to the front foot B extending the arms

SMITHS
ALS
Taunton 74153
SUPPORT SOMERS
g Society
GRI
AYLOR
HARRIS
CLIFTON BRISTOL 8

SMITHS
ALS
Taunton 74153
SUPPORT SOMERSET C.C.C.
ty
GRIBB
AYLOR
HARRIS
CLIFTON BRISTOL 8

C above left: watching the ball as I make contact D below left: rolled wrists

nearly twice as long to score the next fifty, because I took them nearly all in singles, pushing the ball in front of the men spread all around the boundary.

There is a second reason for caution. Not only are you risking being caught by hitting the ball in the air, but you take the chance of being stumped by coming out of your crease with the wicket-keeper standing up. So, when you play the shot, it is even more important to follow the basic rules – your foot to the pitch of the ball, head still, getting behind the line and bringing the bat down straight.

That is obviously going to be impossible if you charge down the wicket running normally – so instead do it by crossing one leg behind the other. Look at the photos overleaf and see that I crossed my right leg behind the left as I advanced down the wicket – literally dancing down. That way when I reached the ball my head remained still, my judgement, control and balance was maintained and I could play with a straight bat. So stay as sideways-on as possible.

There will be times when you try to go down the wicket and realize you have misjudged it – suddenly you can see that you will not get into position to hit the ball cleanly. When that happens simply play with a dead bat, block the ball and regain your ground. If you try to play the shot when you are not in the right position the chances are you will miss it and be stumped.

Because you are taking the double risk of being caught or stumped, you cannot afford anything to go wrong, so save the lofted drive until you have a few runs on the board. Then use it carefully and let everyone enjoy the spectacle.

THE LOFTED DRIVE A below: moving down the wicket

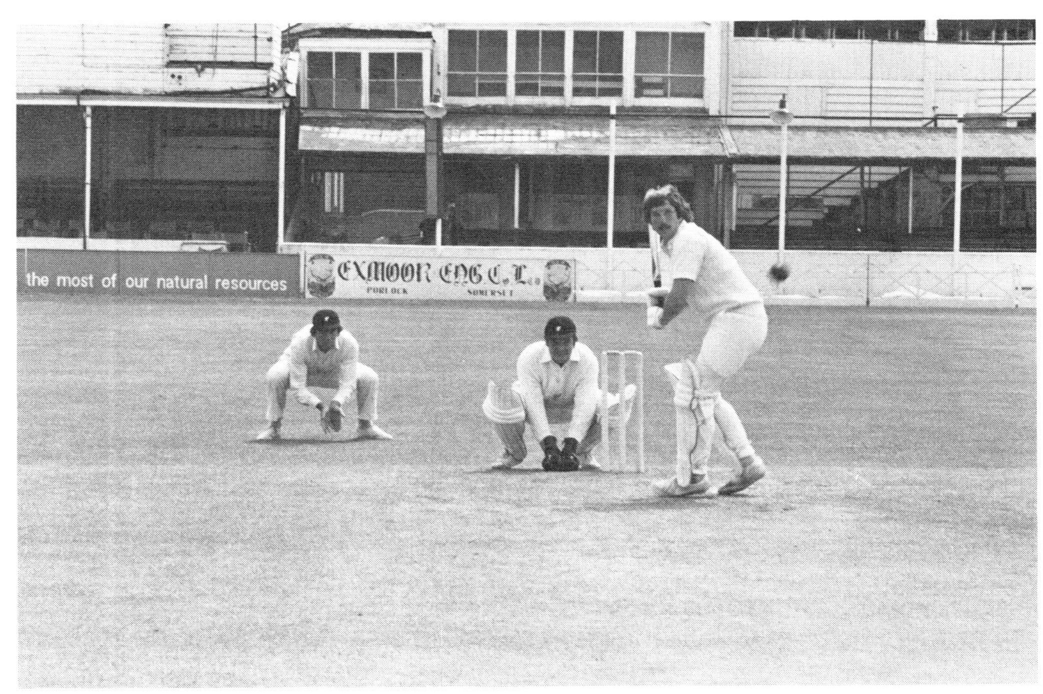

the most of our natural resources
EXMOOR ENG. C. L.
PORLOCK SOMERSET

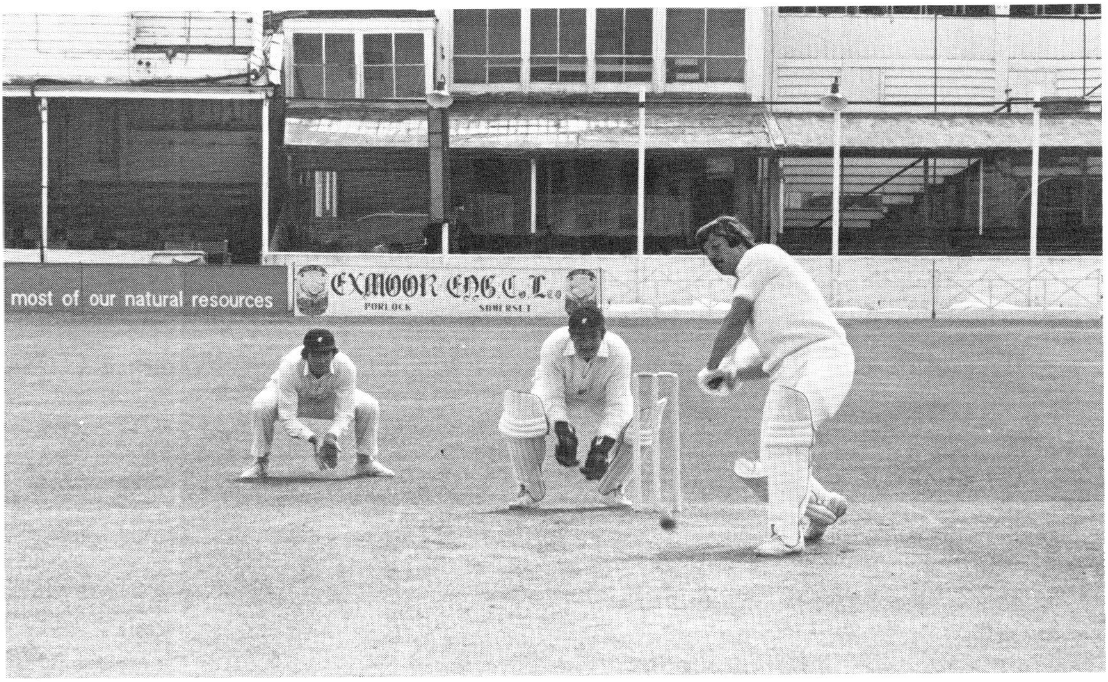
most of our natural resources
EXMOOR ENG. C. L.
PORLOCK SOMERSET

B above left: 'dancing' with right foot crossed behind left
C below left: hit it hard!
D above: follow-through

Chapter 8 **Bowling**

If you want to be a bowler, the worst thing you can do is to start by trying to be a particular type of bowler. Before you start worrying about spin, swing, bouncers, yorkers or seamers you have got to be able to bowl. Just that. A comfortable easy action. A line, and a length.

The reason is that all of the various specialist bowlers in cricket rely on their action to help them. So if you have a good basic action you have a foundation from which to build. You have the important principles mastered.

So start by developing a good, flowing run-up, an easy sideways-on action and a follow-through. Don't try to do it too quickly at first. Fast bowlers are born and not made, and if you have the natural ability to bowl genuinely quickly like Bob Willis it will develop as you grow older – and be even more lethal when it is allied to a perfect action.

Start with the run-up. The keynote here is comfort. You are winding your body up, and the aim is to reach top speed at the wicket in the delivery stride. Don't run too fast at first or you could find you are slowing down as you come to the crease – the complete opposite of what should happen. The run-up should be a gradual acceleration, almost like going through the gears of a car. You start in first gear, almost walking, then second gear takes you into a steady stride. Cruise into third until you are three or four yards from the wicket – then change up again into fourth. All your energy should be concentrated in those last three or four yards. You are winding yourself up like a clockwork toy so that when you release the catch in the delivery stride all the energy explodes.

A lot of schoolboy bowlers develop the bad habit of stopping at the end of their run before they bowl. If they do that they might just as well not have a run. Smoothness is the important thing, so that you make use of the momentum you build up.

Watch the Australian, Dennis Lillee, as a fine example of a player with a smooth, loping run which winds him up perfectly for the fiery delivery stride. Andy Roberts, the West Indian, is another.

Lillee's opening partner, Jeff Thomson, is an interesting contrast as far as the run-up is concerned – and proves the point that it isn't the length of the run-up but how smooth it is that matters. I should think Thommo's run is perhaps only half the length of Lillee's – yet, for my money, he is the quicker bowler. Find the length that is right for you by trial and error, until you are moving easily through the four gears.

The run needs to be an automatic routine. You should work it out, practise it and develop so that you know where your feet go without having to look at them. Then you can concentrate on nothing other than the spot you intend to bowl at. One vital point – keep your head still as you run or you will lose balance.

A lot of fast bowlers develop a very aggressive run-up – something which comes with practice and knowing where your feet are landing without having to look at them. Again, you can compare it to driving a car. A good driver watches the road all the time, rather than looking at the gear lever when he changes it. The West Indian, Michael Holding, is one of the most fearsome examples. He presents an almost terrifying sight, gliding in,

A gathering pace

B a steady run

C into the delivery stride . . . left arm starting to reach up

D right foot lands square to the crease

E the crucial movement of delivery

F follow-through

sure of where his feet are landing, attack written on all his features. I am certain that is worth a few wickets on its own.

The delivery stride is where all that momentum is released. The pictures of my action, from both sideways-on and the batsman's position, give you a good idea of what everything should be doing.

The most difficult thing is moving from running with your chest facing the batsman to bowling in a sideways-on position, with your left hip facing him. But it is absolutely crucial for any type of bowler to master it. As you leap from your left foot, draw your left arm up so that it points almost behind you as you look over your left shoulder at where you are going to bowl. By the time you land on your right foot, everything should be wound up ready to let go. You should be reaching up into the sky with your whole body, pulling yourself up, as you land in the sideways-on position with your right foot roughly parallel with the crease, leaning back slightly, your left leg braced to land with toes pointing towards fine leg.

That is when you deliver the ball. Pull your left arm down and the right arm follows it through like a windmill. Your body should just unwind. Pulling the left arm down and across the body brings the right arm with it. Try to get your bowling arm almost to brush your ear as it comes over, giving yourself the maximum height to make the ball bounce higher.

Try to get everything into the delivery – your back, thighs, arms and shoulders all propelling the ball towards the stumps. Then finish with everything tucked up. Your shoulders go through half a circle in the delivery. They start with the left shoulder facing the batsman and end with the right pointing at him.

Get all that right and you are almost there – but there is still the crucial follow-through. It begins the moment you release the ball, as your right arm follows your left down to the left-hand side of the body. It ends as you cruise off the wicket towards gully, still looking at the batsman all the way.

Don't try to pull up too sharply after you have bowled. Glide into the follow-through. If you try to pull away quickly you will lose your balance, and you might need that for a caught-and-bowled chance. Obviously you cannot run in a straight line, though, because then you would be digging holes in the wicket and would end up in trouble with the umpire for ruining the surface. Aim for gully and you should have no problems.

That basic action is the one which every bowler should use. If you are sideways-on you will always be able to bowl a natural away-swinger, and can then develop an in-swinger to go with it. But a chest-on bowler, although he will be able to move it in towards the batsman, will find it practically impossible to swing it away. It is not only the quicker bowlers trying to swing the ball who need to get that sideways-on action correct. It is equally vital for both types of spinners.

The only other essential quality in a bowler is the ability to maintain accurate line and length. They are overworked words, I know, but what exactly are they? The line is simply explained – it is the direction of the ball – an imaginary line on the ground underneath the ball as it moves through the air. You must be able to control it to attack a batsman's weak points.

A length is harder to explain. You couldn't, for instance, walk on to a wicket and say, 'that is a length'. It varies according to the height of the batsman, whether he likes to play forward or back and the speed of your bowling. The best way to find it is to imagine you are the batsman, about to face your own bowling. Ask yourself where the spot you would least like it to pitch is. That is a good length. It should leave the batsman in two minds, not sure whether to play forward or back, caught in no-man's-land and unable to attack.

When you have mastered the control of a consistent line and length you will almost need nothing else. Tom Cartwright, who was at Somerset when I started playing for the county and is now manager of Glamorgan, used to frustrate people out because his length and direction were so consistent. Mike Hendrick has got the same quality now and it brings him wickets for both Derbyshire and England.

It is a bowler's job to keep the batsman under constant pressure – always worried about what the next ball might do. There is no better way of doing that than constant, accurate bowling

A gathering pace

B a steady run

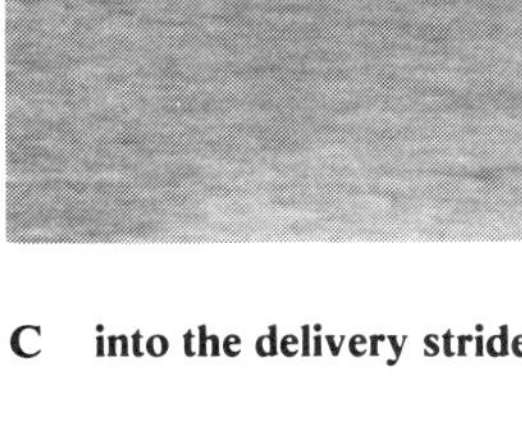

C into the delivery stride

D looking over left shoulder at the batsman

E the delivery

F follow-through

because the batsman knows there is never any escape. When you have got the ability to pin him down like that, you can start working on all the extra shocks and surprises that can be conjured up for him.

It is worth saying that you have to *think* about bowling. Look for the delivery which unsettles a particular batsman, and employ it. It is that element of plotting and planning for success that makes cricket such a good social game. It is certainly why cricketers seem to talk about nothing but cricket. I have spent many an hour discussing the strengths and weaknesses of our opponents – and there is nothing quite to match the feeling of satisfaction when the batsman falls neatly into the trap you prepared for him.

Chapter 9 **The fast bowler**

I suppose every young boy wants to be a fast bowler. He is the glamour man in the attack, a fearsome sight as he runs fluently to the wicket and thunders the ball down at nearly a hundred miles an hour. Batsmen fear his awesome pace and worry at the ball which whistles around their ears.

The problem is that not everyone has the natural ability to bowl quickly. While you can, to some extent, manufacture and coach a batsman or slow bowler out of nothing, a fast bowler either can send the ball flying down with venom or he cannot. And, if he cannot, he will never be a genuine quickie.

I define a fast bowler as somebody who can beat the bat with sheer speed – and there aren't many of them about. Bob Willis is the obvious English example, but I am afraid that most of the other genuine quickies come from overseas – Lillie, Thomson, Hogg, Holding, Roberts, Garner . . . all formidable names. Their great advantage is that they learn to play on hard wickets which help them with good bounce.

I think it is important to remember that none of them are only fast. They are also very accurate. It is certainly true that, without being able to bowl a consistent line and length, it wouldn't matter if you were faster than any of them – you would still be a liability to your team. So the first thing to concentrate on is accuracy. You can develop that in the nets, by practising and practising and practising. I was lucky in that when I was a boy our house in Yeovil backed on to the local boys' school, and the games master, a marvellous man called Fred Hall, used to let me clamber over the fence and join in the net sessions. But you don't really need people to practise with, or expensive equipment, to learn this accuracy. I am sure that near your home you can find a brick wall – and that is all you need. Chalk a wicket on the wall, and then pretend you are the batsman. Decide the length you wouldn't want to face and chalk a circle around it. Then go and bowl, aiming to get the ball to land in that circle and hit the stumps every time.

Whether you have the gift of genuine speed, or are going to bowl medium-pace, that has to be your stock ball. From there you can think about developing some surprise weapons to go with it.

The way to do it, I believe, is to get all the basics of your bowling action correct first. That sideways-on action we talked about in the last chapter is the key. It will give you a natural out-swinger. I have certainly never had to work to bowl an out-swinger – my action is quite good, and it is that which sends the ball swinging away. I do help it, however, with the grip, holding the ball so that the shiny side faces square leg, as you can see in the picture. That helps through aerodynamics. The shiny side of the ball slips through the air more quickly than the rough side, and so steers the ball away from the batsman. Or that, at least, is the theory. I honestly think that if your action was very sideways-on it would still be possible to bowl an out-swinger with the ball held the other way.

It took me much longer to develop an in-swinger. I did it at first by changing my action and bowling chest-on, which helps the ball move into the batsman. The problem was that it was easy to spot the difference. A batsman could see my action change and be prepared for the in-swinger, so the vital element of surprise was lost. Ideally the batsman shouldn't realize the difference until his stumps are flat and he is walking back to the pavilion.

The solution I eventually found was to alter my follow-through. Instead of pulling my left arm down by my left side and letting the right arm follow it, I did the opposite. For my in-swinger now I take my left arm down and across my body to the right, letting the bowling arm follow it there. It wasn't easy to perfect, and at first I found myself losing balance occasionally. But through lots of hard work I can now make the ball go either straight or swing in slightly. It may sound as if I would have been better off sticking to the original chest-on method and getting more swing. But that isn't the case. It is the *surprise* that does the damage and my in-swinger is now much harder for a batsman to spot.

For the in-swinger, of course, I reverse my grip on the ball so that the shiny side is to the off. Again, have a look at the photograph. It is important to hold the ball lightly, so that you merely steer it on its way with the fingers. Gripping the ball tightly means you are not relaxed and you lose some speed.

On the subject of shine, there is nothing which annoys me more than to be given the ball with six marks on it from the previous over. It is everybody's responsibility to look after the shine on the ball, keeping one side gleaming. The harder you work on the ball the more it will do for you. Sweat is very good as a polish. Put some on the ball and then rub hard. As an example of what can be achieved, by the way, the ball I used for the pictures of my grip was given to me looking dull and a tiny bit rough – and you can see that I managed, quite quickly, to make one side of it shine. Even the spinners should take care of the shiny side, because they will occasionally want to deliver a swinging ball.

The other device that quick and medium-pace bowlers use is seam. The object is to make the ball bounce on the seam – and the chances are it will then deviate one way or the other and, if you don't know which, the batsman certainly won't. To do it, hold the ball loosely with your first and second fingers either side of the seam, which should be at right angles to the ground facing the batsman. The lighter your grip on the ball the better your control will be.

The two other variations are a yorker and a bouncer. The yorker is the fast ball which goes as quickly as possible in a straight line from your hand to the stumps. It is a weapon for the fast man more than the medium-pacer, because it beats the batsman by sheer speed. A medium-pacer, however, can still use it effectively, providing he bowls it a fraction quicker than his stock ball.

As for bouncers, I know I have been accused of bowling too many but I think it is something I am curing. I have learnt now that a bouncer, a short ball which rears up dangerously, should only be bowled with the aim of getting a batsman out. You are not trying to hurt the batsman, you are trying to take his wicket. When you get on a wicket where the ball is flying about, it is very tempting to become so excited at how high you can make it leap that you forget why you are bowling in the first place. You have to *think* about it. For instance, in the Prudential World Cup Semi-final against New Zealand in 1979, I think I only bowled one bouncer in my twelve overs. The wicket was slow, and bowling a bouncer would have been asking to be hooked or pulled, so I contained the batsmen by keeping the ball up. But in different circumstances, if I thought I could get a man out with it, I would use it without hesitation. But that has to be the object. Ask yourself what your motive is when you do bowl one. I would stress once more, though, that before you think about bowling bumpers you first have to master the basics.

So let us assume you have polished all that up, and briefly see where you put your fielders. When I am on the attack, early in the innings or if the ball is swinging a lot, I like to fill the slip area. I want at least three slips, a gully, and a short leg in the 'bat-pad' position as my attacking fielders – a cover, fine leg and mid-wicket my defensive men. That leaves me one more man, who would be at leg slip if it was swinging both ways, or fourth slip. You will notice that I have not got a mid-off. That is because I want the batsman to try to hit me through there. If the ball is swinging, that is the shot which will give edges.

If I don't get a breakthrough, then I would take

The out-swinger

The in-swinger

my fourth slip to mid-off, and drop the 'bat-pad' man back to square leg – and as time wore on my third slip would go out to third man. Normally I like to keep two slips and, with patience, plugging away on my line and length outside the off-stump, there is a good chance that the batsman could eventually offer a catch.

Finally, patience is a vital quality. When things are not going well and the wicket is good, little variations combined with a consistent line and length will get best results. Try to make the batsman lose his control before you lose yours.

Chapter 10 **The off-spinner**

A spin bowler lives on his wits and cunning. He has to make the batsman think, bring him forward, force him back, tempt him, trick him. He uses turn and flight to beat the bat – creeping in through the side door while the fast bowler is trying to batter down the wall.

I think a good off-spinner nags people out. By that I mean that he bowls such a constant tight line and length, that the batsman eventually tries to force runs which are not there. That is when he plays a bad shot and the spinner is in.

To be able to do that you have to develop a good stock ball. Four or five balls of every over will be identical off-breaks, pitching around off-stump and turning in. It is done by flicking the ball with the first two fingers. Grip the ball with the seam running across the two fingers, as in the photographs overleaf, and flick the two across each other to gain the spin. It is the index finger which does most of the work.

If you look at the photo of my Somerset team-mate, Vic Marks, bowling you will see that it is the index finger which is last to make contact with the ball. To help you master this 'flicking' technique, spend idle moments spinning a cricket ball into the air and catching it, trying to make it spin as much as you can. Master that technique and then work hard to get your line and length. Again, at first, a good basic action and accuracy is more important to you than trying to spin the ball too much, or trying all sorts of variations.

Like any bowler, your run-up has to be comfortable. That means that you can go through the delivery effortlessly, even when you want to slip in a quicker ball. The key is to drop into a rhythm – the same smooth, relaxed movement every ball. Spinners often have to bowl long spells, and unless you have got this relaxed approach and delivery you will find it difficult. Your action is very important, because a lot of the spin comes from the body. The aim is to pivot on your straight left leg, twisting your body so that your studs cut a circle in the turf.

A fast bowler likes to get a batsman playing on his back foot, but an off-spinner should normally drop into a length which brings the batsman forward. You will not get many wickets on good pitches when people play back to you. Indeed, it is worth saying that you should not worry too much if you get driven over your head. That was a good ball – and the batsman had to hit it in the air to score runs, which always gives you a chance. You can set a field for it. The time to start asking yourself questions is when you are pulled or cut. That is just rank bad bowling.

When you have achieved your first priority and developed a good stock ball, that is the time to think about adding some variety to your repertoire. The most lethal relies on your action being correct. By being sideways-on you can bowl an out-swinger – a ball which swings on towards slip rather than turning into the batsman. It is most effective bowled on leg-stump, where it tempts the batsman to sweep, and gives you a chance of getting a top edge. The secret is that it looks at first like a bad ball.

Another way to give this false illusion of a bad ball is with the flighted delivery. It should take an arc slightly higher than the stock ball, but pitch a foot or two shorter. It looks like a full toss, until it dips late and will get the batsman either playing over the ball or hitting in the air. Swop that with

above: Grip for the off-break

right: The index finger puts the spin on the ball

6
29
5
38
WLER 4
CAUGHT 9

the quicker one which can beat a batsman for pace simply because he is not expecting it.

It is important that the difference between all these deliveries and your stock ball should be only minimal. There is no point tossing the ball high into the air – it is obviously a slower delivery. Disguise it. The best off-spinners bowl their slower ball by whipping the arm over quickly but letting the ball go over the top of the hand, rather than out of the side. It looks like a quick full toss to the batsman; it is actually a slow, short ball.

On a bad pitch it is normal to bowl round the wicket. If you continued to bowl over on a turning pitch the ball would be going down the leg side after it turned, and you couldn't hope to get an l.b.w. decision. The solution is to bowl round the wicket, so that the ball pitches on middle stump and straightens to hit it.

Bowling round the wicket is also a useful tactic on good wickets to present the batsman with different problems. It means he is having to cope with a different line of attack. Never let a batsman relax – keep him worried all the time by setting all sorts of different traps. Then be patient and with luck he will fall into one.

As for an off-spinner's field settings, on good wickets it is normal to start with a five-four field, a slip and three men in the covers, with the rest on the leg side. On turning wickets crowd the batsman with a leg slip, forward short leg and silly point. The point and two men in the covers will be your only off-side fielders – if you get hit behind the wicket on the off-side it means you have bowled a bad ball, and you shouldn't set fields for bad balls.

When the pitch is wet and taking turn, resist the temptation to try to spin the ball a lot. It may be exciting to see it turn and jump, but it is even more crucial under these conditions to concentrate on a line and length. If the ball is turning you will not need to work hard to help it and, if you keep it on a length, something will happen of its own accord.

Chapter 11 **The leg-spinner**

Leg-spin is probably the hardest art to master in cricket. There are only a handful of leg-spinners left in English cricket – and I cannot honestly see it being easy for a leg-spinner to make a career in first-class cricket purely on his bowling in the future.

But, and it is a very big but, it is a wonderful second string for a good batsman to add to his bow. I am sure any captain would like to have a leg-spinner available to vary the attack at some time – and if I had to choose between two very good batsmen when I was picking a team, I would always go for the one who could bowl as well.

The reason that English leg-spinners have died out is the poor quality of most wickets. They tend to be slow and not give much bounce – and it is the extra bounce which makes a leg-spinner so difficult to play. On a slow wicket he has got no margin of error. In Australia, where the wickets are normally harder, many club sides have got two leg-spinners, and it is the off-spinner who is practically unheard of. Jim Higgs was one of the most difficult bowlers to face during our Ashes winning tour. But I believe he would struggle in a full season in England.

All that said, I would encourage anybody who wants to try leg-spinning to give it a go. It is tremendous fun and, allied to good batting, could give you real prospects in the first-class game. That is the combination which my Somerset team-mate, Peter Roebuck, who helped me write this chapter, possesses, and I believe he has a very big future.

The most important principle is that the leg-spinner gets his spin from the wrist, rather than the fingers. It is this which makes leg-spinning so difficult. Making the ball turn is one thing, but combining it with line and length, another task altogether.

So the first thing to master is the snappy wrist action. It requires a very strong wrist. Practise it by taking a ball – or an orange, or apple, or anything the size of a cricket ball – and gripping it loosely in the ends of your fingers. Hold the ball, fruit or whatever, with your palm facing the ground and fingers pointing down – then flick it into the air and catch it again, keeping the arm still. To do that, you will see, you have to snap the wrist sharply backwards. At first you will find the ball will go all over the place – which could perhaps leave you in trouble for bruising all the best fruit! But do not be deterred, keep practising it and slowly you will build control. Make sure the snap is a complete movement – the fingers pointing first to the floor then to the ceiling.

If your hands are small this is not easy. In fact, you do need big hands to be a leg-spinner, which means that until you are thirteen or fourteen you will not be able to bowl leg-breaks. Until then, bowl medium-pacers, so that you learn the principles of line and length and develop a good action.

And as a leg-spinner you will need a *perfect* action. You need a more sideways-on position than anybody else, bowling the ball from behind almost like a javelin thrower, and getting your arm exceptionally high at the moment of delivery. It means you have got to get all these basics right from an early stage.

A leg-spinner's action is not very fast. In fact,

THE LEG-BREAK **The wrist cracks at the moment of delivery**

until the moment of delivery it looks almost like slow motion. But then comes the crack of the wrist whipping across to deliver the ball. As the bowling arm comes up the fingers are pointing to mid-on – as the ball leaves the hand they should point to mid-off. It will take years of practice to master this technique. You can expect to be at least thirty before you reach your peak.

When you have got the leg-break under control it is time to develop the googly – which looks the same to the batsman but, in fact, turns into him rather than away. It is, in fact bowled more with the fingers than the wrist. Study the pictures of Pete bowling the googly, compare them with the leg-break and I will try to explain what he does. You will have seen that for the normal leg-break the wrist snaps from out to in. For the googly the ball comes round the side of the hand. It begins with the back of the hand facing the batsman, and is bowled by twisting the arm round as much as possible to get the spin. You can see that Pete's arm is under terrific strain in the googly because it is twisted right round. The aim, as ever, is disguise. It looks to the batsman like a leg-break, but turns the other way. Bowling that against a batsman who cannot pick it is enormous fun because you soon get him terribly jittery. At school level you should be able to destroy the tail-end because they just won't be able to read the change in turn. You will find the googly is probably a bit slower than your stock leg-break. The number of people

THE GOOGLY The arm twists round and the ball comes from the side of the hand

who can bowl both at the same pace is very small.

The other variation is even more deadly to batsmen – but unfortunately even more difficult to bowl. It is the top-spinner, or 'flipper' as it is sometimes called. It gains pace off the pitch and rather than turning one way or the other, it hurries straight on. The ball should come over the top of the hand, but beyond that it is difficult to say more about how to bowl it – it seems to be a very individual thing. The answer is trial and error until you discover it. Suddenly you will manage to do it, and then again and again. The flipper is the most dangerous ball of all, because it comes so quickly it gives the batsman no time to adjust. A googly comes off the pitch more slowly, because it is not a wrist ball. But the flipper absolutely fizzes through. A lot of people get bowled trying to cut it. They go back to give themselves room, but, instead of turning away, it hurries on and beats them for pace.

The most common mistake young leg-spinners make is trying to hit the stumps by pitching outside leg and turning back in. A good batsman will sweep that ball or just kick it away. If it is outside the leg-stump it is a free ball. Aim to pitch around middle stump, and one or two that do not turn so much will still take off-stump. It is also important when bowling both leg-break and googly, to pitch on the same spot. There would be no point pitching your leg-break on leg-stump all the time, and googly on off-stump, because it destroys the disguise.

A normal field setting will be predominantly off-side, with mid-on, mid-wicket, deep backward square leg and short fine leg on the on-side, and a mid-off, extra cover, cover, point and slip on the off.

My last piece of advice to budding leg-spinners is be philosophical. It is great fun, so regard it in that light. Some days you will take a lot of wickets, others you will concede a lot of runs. Unlike an off-spinner, you will find it hard to maintain a constant tight line and length to contain a batsman. You are an attacking bowler, trying to take wickets. Be patient and persistent, and wear a smile.

Chapter 12 **Wicket-keeping**

Wicket-keepers are like fast bowlers. They are born, not made. They need almost perfect balance, a very safe pair of hands and an early start, then good coaching to bring out their natural ability.

I think anybody with ball sense could do an adequate job standing back to the quicker bowlers. But the test of a good wicket-keeper is that he is still in command when he moves up to the stumps to take the spinners or slower medium-pace bowlers. Then you have to be able to move correctly and quickly – you can have the safest pair of hands in the world but it is no use if you don't get them to the ball.

Let us start with the most basic question, where and how do you stand? It must be either back or up. In so many club games you see the wicket-keeper lost in no-man's-land, which is the worst mistake. Stood back, you should be able to take the ball as it is starting to loop down for its second bounce. Never stand where the ball is rising. Stood up, get right behind the stumps – you can see the position demonstrated by Somerset's wicket-keeper, Derek Taylor, in the photographs. His left leg is between middle and off-stump, giving him a clear view round the batsman at the ball. Never stand behind the wicket because your vision is obstructed. You always need to see the bowler and ball easily. Derek's weight is balanced equally on the balls of either foot, with his hands together and fingers pointing down. Your fingers should always point either down or up – never towards the bowler.

Settle in your stance, and the next problem is when should you come up from that low position? The best way is to rise with the ball. In other words, stay down in your stance until the ball pitches, then come up with it to the same height as the bounce. It is easier to come up than to get back down again. Never give any ball up. Go through the motions of taking it even after the batsman has played the ball. That is something which you will see illustrated by Derek in all the pictures in the batting section of this book.

The best way to move to take the ball is shown in the two photograph sequences of Derek stumping me. The first shows him taking the ball on the off-side, which is the easiest. Derek says he always tries to keep his weight on his left leg when he takes the ball outside the off-stump. It was a method which Arthur McIntyre, the brilliant former Surrey and England wicket-keeper, taught him. There is a school of thought which recommends moving round in a semi-circle, transferring the weight to the right foot. But Derek finds his method makes it more easy to ride with the ball if it comes through quickly, and to keep his position to get back to the stumps to whip the bails off if there is a stumping chance.

More difficult is the leg-side stumping, because for a second you are blind as the batsman is between you and the ball. Try to anticipate the pitch and bounce of the ball and get in position for it. That is partly the reason why you should go through the motions of taking every ball, even when the batsman has hit it. It makes the act of sensing the pitch of the ball automatic. When the ball is down the leg-side, move to get it with your weight on your right leg, again helping you to ride with the ball and get back to the bails quickly.

Do not be over-ambitious about standing up to the stumps, especially on bad pitches. It will soon

The stance

OFF-SIDE STUMPING A above: the stance
B above right: coming up with the ball
C below right: both hands together

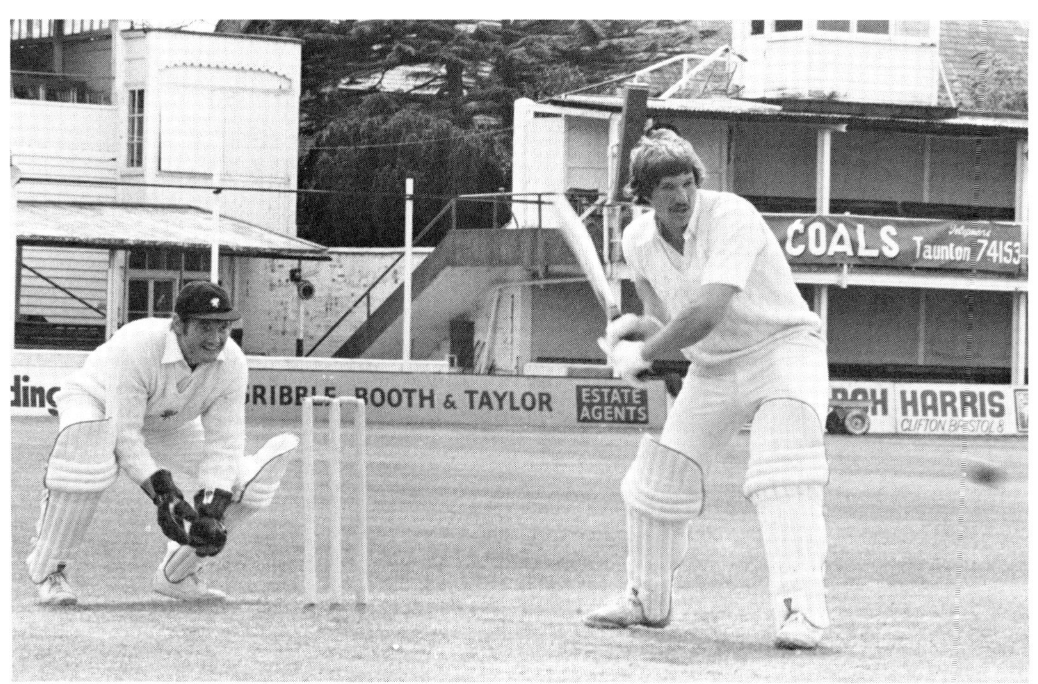

COALS
Taunton 74153
GRIBBLE BOOTH & TAYLOR
ESTATE AGENTS
HARRIS
CLIFTON BRISTOL 8

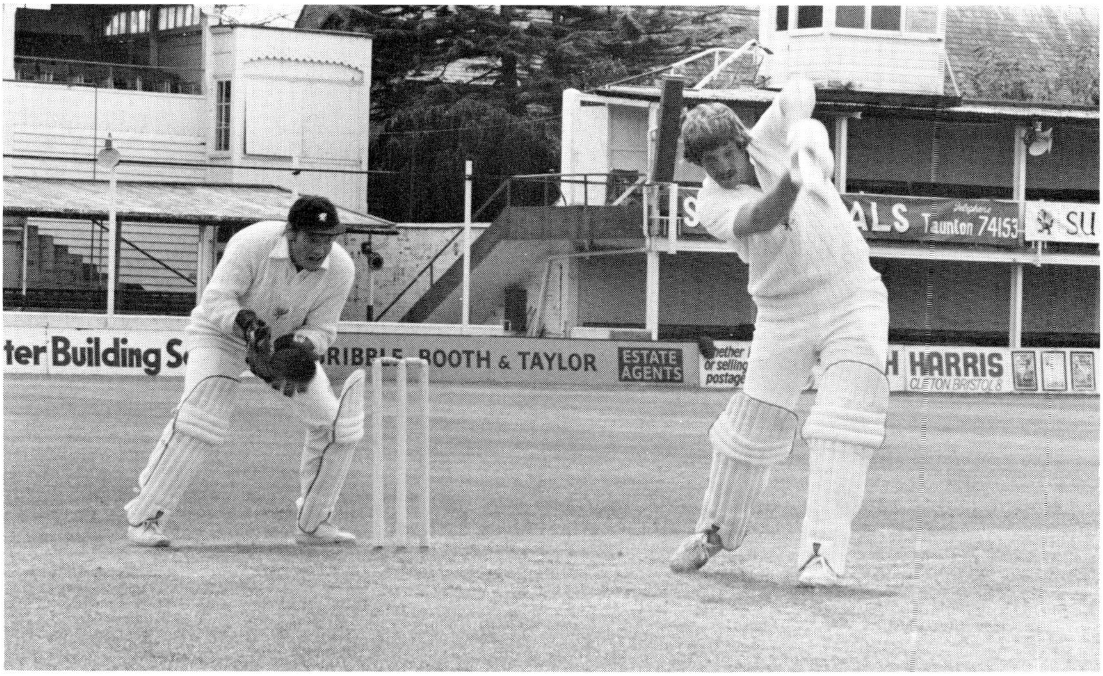
ALS
Taunton 74153
ter Building S
GRIBBLE BOOTH & TAYLOR
ESTATE AGENTS
HARRIS
CLIFTON BRISTOL 8

D whip the bails off quickly

ruin your confidence, because you will never know where the ball is going. But, when you can, standing up helps the bowler a good deal. It gives him a bigger target, and it stops the batsman taking liberties by moving his guard outside the crease. Derek likes to stand up to our medium-pacers whenever he can – but even he has the sense to go back on very bad pitches.

It is important for a youngster to learn to keep wicket on good pitches. One of the problems is that much club cricket is played on poor surfaces, which gives a promising youngster no chance. I should think, if it is possible, an artificial pitch is best to start with, because it gives an even bounce. It is always difficult for a wicket-keeper to get good practice. A lot just go into the nets and keep behind all the different bowlers. But it is best to go with one bowler at a time. You know how he bowls, what his variations are, and you can concentrate solely on that job – just as in a match you receive six balls at a time from one bowler. That is asking a lot of the other fellows, because they have their own practice to do. But, if you are dedicated to wicket-keeping, it is the best way.

The wicket-keeper has a big responsibility to the fielders. Generally, the better he plays the better the team will field. It is up to him to get up behind the stumps as quickly as possible to take the fielder's throw so that he is in position for a possible run out. The most difficult throw to take is one that comes in on the half-volley in front of you. Then apply the same rule that you use to take any delivery from the bowler. Stay down low behind the stumps until the ball bounces, then come up with it.

Let the slip fielders do their job. It is up to you to tell them where to stand, and to decide which catches you go for and which are for them. There is nothing more annoying when you are in the slips than going for a catch and then having the wicket-keeper diving in front of you and putting you off.

A quick word on equipment: it is very important to look after your gloves, and wear a pair of chamois leather, or cotton, inners. You must always wear a box and pads for protection – but the pads are really only for extra safety. If you do the job properly you should never be hit on the legs. Always take the ball in your gloves, not using the pads to block it. A wicket-keeper using his pads is a sure sign that he is coming up out of his stance too early.

A last point: everybody has good and bad days. When things are not going well try to relax. When your hands get tight because you are nervous they seem to develop springs in them. Your hands have to give with the ball when you catch it, and they cannot do that if they are not relaxed.

LEG-SIDE STUMPING The weight stays on Derek's right foot all the time. It doesn't move, which means he always knows where the stumps are

HTI Services
Conditioning
Bristol & West Building Society

HTI Services
West Building Society

Chapter 13 **The captain**

The captain is the man who turns eleven individuals into a team. He is the leader, the man who organizes and orchestrates the side. He has an almost impossible job – to please everybody and get results.

The hardest job for a captain is separating himself from the excitement of a match to make calm, logical decisions. He has to develop an impartial view of the game and do what he thinks is right for the team. He has to ignore personal friendships or dislikes and work to get the best out of everybody.

A captain needs a calm tactical mind. His object is to keep the other side under constant pressure – giving them fresh problems every time they seem to have got settled. It means he must be experienced and knowledgeable, as well as a good judge of conditions and other people's performances.

Team spirit is totally the captain's responsibility. The talent he needs most is the ability to handle personalities – to know that one player needs quiet encouragement while another needs a rocket. He has got to solve the dressing-room arguments, and at the same time make sure that any disagreements stay *in* the dressing-room and don't get taken onto the field. A good team comprises eleven individuals trying their hardest for the sake of the others. It seems that two people chase every ball to the boundary, and there is always somebody backing up a wild throw. The batting seems resolute and difficult to dominate, and there is always somebody who wants to bowl. In fact, when the chips are down, you can always seem to rely on somebody to come up with a battling individual performance to rescue things. And, if the side is beaten, it certainly is not from lack of trying. In any side, that collective will-to-win is a vital quality. Good sides who start arguing among themselves become bad sides. Not only that, it is simply more fun to play in a happy team.

A captain has to get the best out of the players he has available. At Somerset I have watched while our captain, Brian Rose – who incidentally helped me write this chapter – has persuaded people who didn't seem to have a hope of making it that they have got ability. That confidence has brought them on 500 per cent. Suddenly they take the field believing they are better than, or at least as good as, anyone they are playing against.

Again, it all goes back to handling personalities – the ability to understand people and to know what makes them tick, to see what they are capable of and instil in them the desire to achieve their best. A captain has to cajole, coach, demand and discipline his men.

It is discipline that I think is the key. Brian Close, Somerset's previous captain, was a tough disciplinarian. He made us a hard side, with an edge of steel – and was prepared to kick people up the backside who thought they were too good for that. But I think he found it hard to get over to players what he wanted them to do – and he wouldn't ask you to do anything he couldn't do or hadn't done. Brian Rose has taken that to another stage. He likes self-discipline. As he says: 'If I have to tell somebody off I have failed in my job. They should know the right thing to do, and want to do it.'

I think there is a lot of truth in that. Most people know when they have made a mistake and they didn't intend to. In these circumstances it is better to laugh it off rather than rant and rave and create ill-feeling. I think the only time there is any justification for that is when people don't even try. Then they deserve everything they get because they are a liability to everybody else in the team.

If you are not prepared to take responsibility, then you will not make a captain. You need confidence in your own judgements – to be able to make a decision and stick by it. That doesn't mean, however, that you don't listen to other people's opinions and take advice. As a bowler I like to have a good harmony with my captain on where my fielders should be, or how best to attack a batsman. There is nothing more annoying than the bloke who sets a field how he wants it, then leaves you to get on and bowl. When that happens you are getting mad at your own captain, rather than at the opposition, which is self-defeating. If we differ in an opinion, Brian will always offer to try my way if his doesn't seem to be getting any results in an over or two. I think that is good management, and it is very rare for us to have any major disagreement.

The most complete captain I have played under is Mike Brearley. Oddly, though, it was an Australian, Rodney Hogg, who summed him up best. 'That man,' he said, 'has got a degree in people.' That is what good captaincy is about.

I hope the tips I have given you in this book might go some way towards helping you get a 'degree' in cricket. Try hard. It is a wonderful game.

Glossary

Appeal 'How's that?' by any fieldsman invites the umpires to decide whether either batsman is 'out' under any law of cricket. In practice any noise or vigorous hand movement is recognized by umpires as an appeal and it may be made up until the time the next ball is bowled, unless an interval intervenes.

Backing up (a) Non-striker moving a couple of paces up the pitch in case a run is possible.
(b) One fielder moving behind another to cut off a scoring stroke in case his team-mate fails to do so. It is important to back up a wicket-keeper against inaccurate return throws.

Bails Two bails, each $4\frac{3}{8}$ inches long, which rest in grooves at the top of the stumps. The bails separate three stumps and together they form the wicket. A bail must be completely removed from the top of the stumps for the wicket to be down.

Ball Spherical shaped with cork interior bound with twine. Covered with red leather, two halves joined at the seam, the circumference must be between $8\frac{13}{16}$ and 9 inches and the weight between $5\frac{1}{2}$ and $5\frac{3}{4}$ oz.

Bat Must not be more than $4\frac{1}{4}$ inches wide or 38 inches long. The usual weight is between 2 lb. 4 oz. and 2 lb. 6 oz. Made of willow with a cane handle.

Beamer A fast full toss at head height which can frighten some batsmen.

Bosie Nickname for the googly, a right-hand bowler's off-break, delivered seemingly with a leg-break action. Otherwise a 'wrong 'un'. Named after B. J. T. Bosanquet (Middlesex and England), who first used it.

Bye Run scored when the ball passes the wicket without touching bat or batsman.

Carry one's bat When an opening bat remains not-out at the fall of the last wicket.

Chinaman An off-break bowled by a left-handed wrist-spin bowler, first perfected by Eddie Achong, West Indies bowler of Chinese extraction.

Chinese cut An unintentional snick which passes perilously near to the leg stump on its way down to long leg.

Chop A late cut made with the bat moving downwards.

Cow-shot Hit from off to leg across the flight of the ball made with a horizontal bat. Disliked by purists.

Daisy cutter A grub or shooter. A delivery which does not rise as much as expected after pitching.

Dead ball The ball is dead (a) when finally settled in the bowler's or wicket-keeper's hands, (b) when it crosses the boundary, (c) when lodged in the batsman's or umpire's clothing, (d) when 'over' is called, (e) when a batsman is 'out', (f) when the bails fall off before delivery, (g) when the bowler accidentally drops the ball before delivery.

Declaration A captain can declare the innings closed at any time except in an English County match reduced to one day when a side must bat for at least an hour. A captain can forfeit his second innings in County cricket.

Draw (a) an undecided match or (b) a deflected stroke to long leg between the legs.

Duck No score by the batsman.

Flipper Top spinner bowled by a right-handed leg-break bowler. It hurries through without deviation and can trap a batsman l.b.w.

Full pitch Ball which can be played before it bounces.

Gate Gap between bat and pad through which a batsman of poor technique is often bowled.

Guard Mark on the crease given by the umpire from behind the bowler's wicket to the batsman in relation to the stumps.

Hat-trick Three wickets in three successive deliveries by one bowler. This qualifies, even if it is in two different games.

In-swinger Delivery from a right-handed bowler which moves in the air from off to leg into a right-handed batsman.

Jack No. 11 batsman. Last three in the batting order are 9, 10, jack.

Late cut A stroke played with the wrists to a

ball outside the off-stump which, off the back foot, sends it speeding through the slips.

Leg-bye Run scored when the ball touches batsman (except his hands). The batsman must have tried to hit the ball.

Leg-cutter A leg-break by a fastish bowler bowled by cutting across the seam.

Length (a good length). Ball pitched so that the batsman is uncertain whether to play forward or backwards.

Long handle An attacking batsman scoring quickly is said to use the long handle.

Long hop A bad ball so short that it can be easily hit for four.

Maiden An over off which no run is scored.

Nelson Most famous sailor with one arm, one eye and one inflexible ambition for victory. Cricketers call the score 111 the Nelson and 333 the Triple Nelson.

New ball May be taken at the commencement of each team's innings and after 85 overs have been bowled. Popularly known as 'a cherry', the new ball usually swings more than a used one.

No ball The batsman is exempt from dismissal, bowled, caught, stumped or l.b.w. from it. If no runs are scored one run (extra) is added to the score. The umpire at the bowler's end will call and signal 'no ball' if the bowler in his delivery stride oversteps the mark, or if the bowler, unannounced, changes from overs to lobs, or from over the wicket to round the wicket or vice-versa. The umpire at square leg will call and signal 'no ball' if there are more than two on-side fielders behind the popping crease. Either umpire signals 'no ball' by extending one arm horizontally. No ball does not count as a delivery.

Off-break Ball which turns from off to leg after pitching. The bowler spins the ball with the right-hand index finger while turning his wrist clockwise.

Off-cutter Fast off-break bowled by cutting across the seam instead of using finger spin.

Out-swinger A ball which moves from leg to off through the air. The ball goes with the arm.

Over the wicket Bowler delivers the ball with the arm which is nearest the stumps.

Pair Batsman out for nought twice in a match. King pair: out *first* ball twice in a match.

Pitch Playing area 22 yards long and 5 feet wide on either side of a line joining the centre of the wickets. Should be used throughout the match. Bowlers must refrain from damaging it.

Playing back (a) A stroke to a short ball. The batsman moves his foot nearest the stumps back and transfers his weight to it.

(b) Second look at the TV film of any incident.

Pop A sharply lifting ball 'pops' off the pitch.

Popping crease Line 4 feet in front and parallel to bowling crease. Batsman wholly outside it could be stumped or run out.

Retired Batsman may discontinue his innings at any time. If he is ill or injured he *may* resume at the fall of a wicket with the consent of the opposing captain.

Round the wicket Bowler delivers the ball with the arm which is furthest from the stumps.

Seamer Bowler who aims to pitch the ball on the seam and then to move it after pitching.

Shine Smooth polished surface of the ball when new, which some bowlers seek to retain by polishing the ball on their trousers or shirt.

Silly fielder Point, mid-on or mid-off who are perilously close to the batsman.

Sweep Stroke played with horizontal bat moving in a semi-circle across the line of the ball pitching near the leg stump. Gathers many runs but causes purists to have apoplexy.

Ton A century, three figures, one hundred runs or more.

Umpires Must see that wickets are properly pitched. They interpret the laws and ensure that all playing equipment conforms to the laws. An umpire may alter his decision if he does so promptly, but once settled his decision is final.

Wide Ball so high or wide when it passes the batsman that it is out of his reach when he has taken a normal guard.

Yorker A full length ball which is intended to go under the bat as the batsman plays forward. Can surprise a batsman starting his innings.